Bradley's Big Note ★
FOUR STAR POPS
Arranged by Richard Bradley

MW00683215

Richard Bradley is one of the world's best known and largest selling arrangers of piano music for print. His success can be attributed to Richard's years of experience as a teacher, and his understanding of students' and players' needs. His innovative piano methods for adults ("Bradley's How To Play Piano" – Adult Books 1, 2 and 3) and kids ("Bradley For Kids" – Red, Blue and Green Series) not only teach the instrument, they teach musicanship each step of the way.

Originally from the Chicago area, Richard completed his undergraduate and graduate work at the Chicago Conservatory of Music and Roosevelt University. After college, Richard became a print arranger for Hansen Publications, and later became Music Director of Columbia Pictures Publications. In 1977, he co-founded his own publishing company, Bradley Publications, which is now exclusively distributed world-wide by Warner Bros. Publications.

Richard is equally well known for his piano workshops, clinics and teacher training seminars. He was a panelist for the first and second Keyboard Teachers' National Video Conferences, which were attended by more than 20,000 piano teachers throughout the United States.

The home video version of his adult teaching method, "How To Play Piano With Richard Bradley", was nominated for an American Video Award as Best Music Instruction Video, and, with sales climbing each year since its release, it has brought thousands of adults to –– or back to –– piano lessons. Still, Richard advises, "The video can only get an adult started and show them what they can do. As they advance, all students need direct input from an accomplished teacher."

Additional Richard Bradley videos aimed at other than the beginning pianist include "How To Play Blues Piano" and "How To Play Jazz Piano". As a frequent television talk show guest on the subject of music education, Richard's many appearances include "Hour Magazine" with Gary Collins, "The Today Show", and "Mother's Day" with "Good Morning America" host Joan Lunden, as well as dozens of local shows.

Bradley
Publications
a division of
RBR Communications, Inc.

– Contents –

AT THE BEGINNING (from "Anastasia")
  – Richard Marx and Donna Lewis ★★★★ 26
BECAUSE YOU LOVED ME
  – Celine Dion ★★★★ 52
BLESSED
  – Elton John ★★★★ 110
BLUE
  – LeAnn Rimes ★★★★ 174
BREAKFAST AT TIFFANY'S
  – Deep Blue Something ★★★★ 184
BUTTERFLY KISSES
  – Bob Carlisle ★★★★ 15
DREAMING OF YOU
  – Selena ★★★★ 188
FOLLOW YOU DOWN
  – Gin Blossoms ★★★★ 57
FOR YOU I WILL
  – Monica ★★★★ 31
THE GIFT
  – Jim Brickman, Collin Raye and Susan Ashton ★★★★ 160
HARD TO SAY I'M SORRY
  – Az Yet Featuring Peter Cetera ★★★★ 48
HERO
  – Mariah Carey ★★★★ 155
HOW DO I LIVE
  – LeAnn Rimes ★★★★ 10
I BELIEVE I CAN FLY
  – R. Kelly ★★★★ 92
I BELIEVE IN YOU AND ME
  – Whitney Houston ★★★★ 75
(Everything I Do) I DO IT FOR YOU
  – Bryan Adams ★★★★ 178
I DON'T WANT TO
  – Toni Braxton ★★★★ 128
I LOVE YOU ALWAYS FOREVER
  – Donna Lewis ★★★★ 62
I SWEAR
  – All-For-One ★★★★ 169
I WILL ALWAYS LOVE YOU
  – Whitney Houston ★★★★ 103

KILLING ME SOFTLY (With His Song)
   – Fugees ★★★★ 142
NOW AND FOREVER
   – Richard Marx ★★★★ 80
PLEASE FORGIVE ME
   – Bryan Adams ★★★★ 138
QUIT PLAYING GAMES (With My Heart)
   – Backstreet Boys ★★★★ 22
REACH
   – Gloria Estefan ★★★★ 120
RUN TO YOU
   – Whitney Houston ★★★★ 133
SAY YOU'LL BE THERE
   – Spice Girls ★★★★ 36
SOMEBODY'S CRYING
   – Chris Isaak ★★★★ 88
SOMETHING ABOUT THE WAY YOU LOOK TONIGHT
   – Elton John ★★★★ 4
THE SWEETEST DAYS
   – Vanessa Williams ★★★★ 150
TEARS IN HEAVEN
   – Eric Clapton ★★★★ 116
UN–BREAK MY HEART
   – Toni Braxton ★★★★ 68
THE WIND BENEATH MY WINGS
   – Bette Midler ★★★★ 124
WITHOUT YOU
   – Mariah Carey ★★★★ 84
WORDS GET IN THE WAY
   – Gloria Estefan ★★★★ 146
YOU GOT IT
   – Bonnie Raitt ★★★★ 98
YOU LIGHT UP MY LIFE
   – LeAnn Rimes ★★★★ 72
YOU MEAN THE WORLD TO ME
   – Toni Braxton ★★★★ 164
YOU WERE MEANT FOR ME
   – Jewel ★★★★ 42
YOU'LL SEE
   – Madonna ★★★★ 106

SOMETHING ABOUT THE WAY
YOU LOOK TONIGHT

Recorded by Elton John

Music by ELTON JOHN
Lyrics by BERNIE TAUPIN
Arranged by Richard Bradley

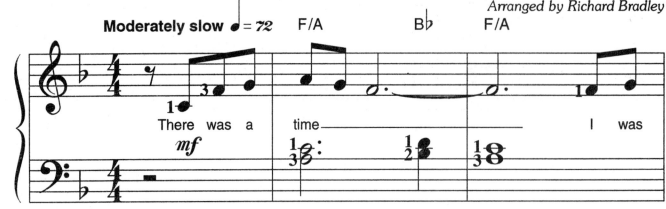

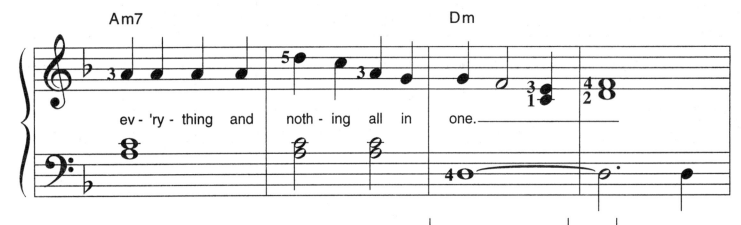

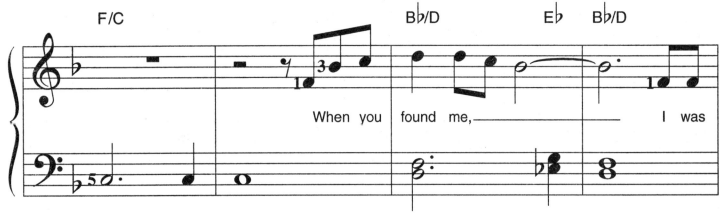

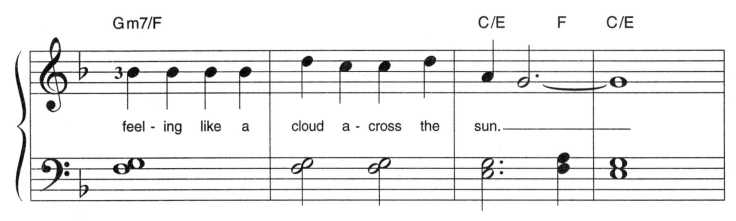

Something About The Way You Look Tonight - 6 - 1

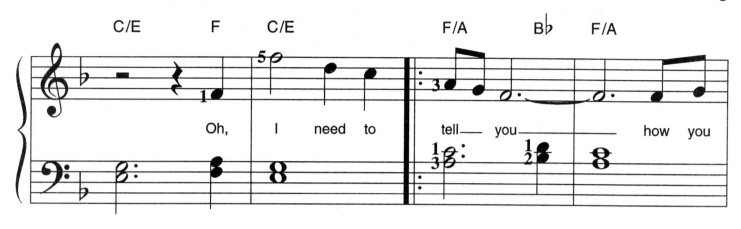

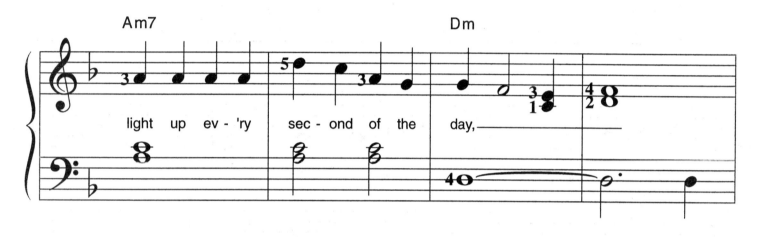

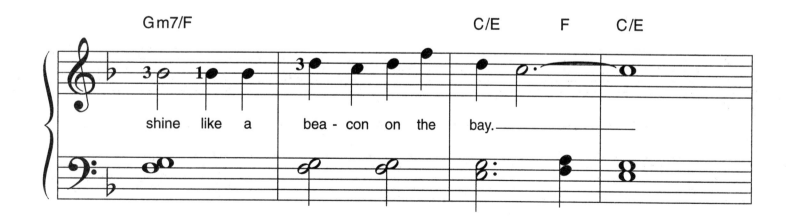

6

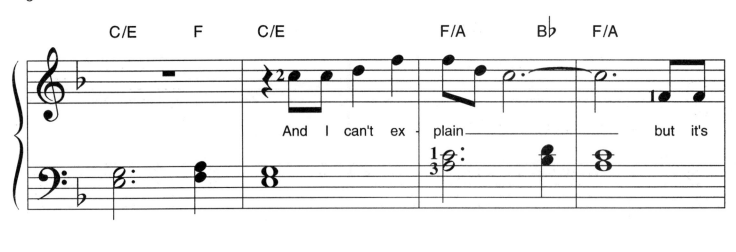

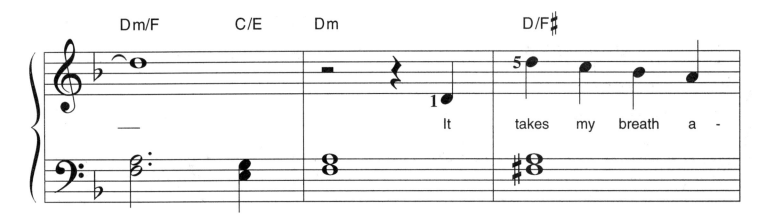

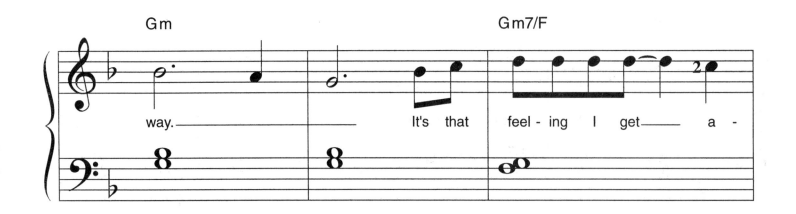

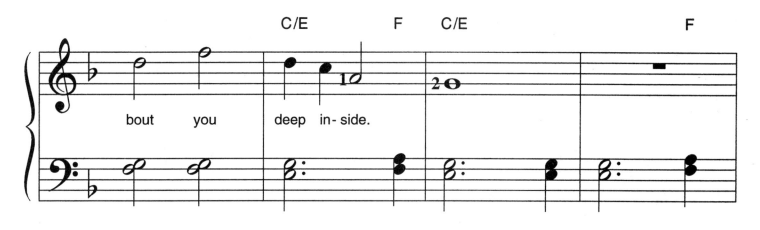

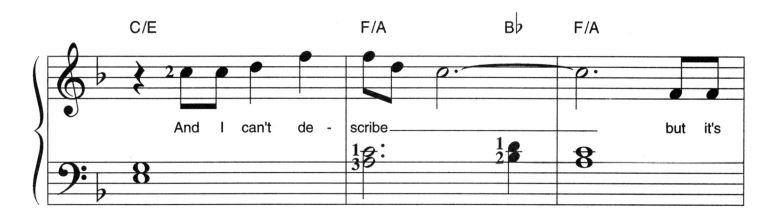

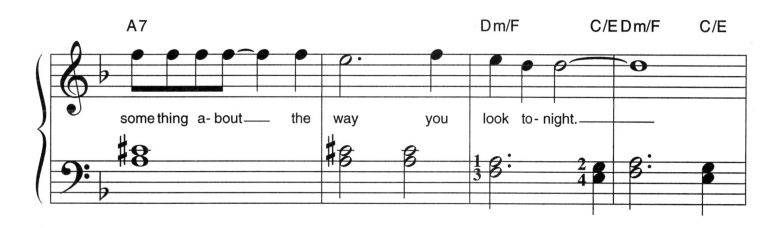

8

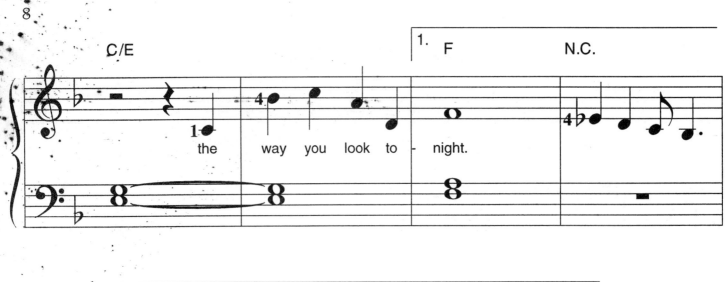

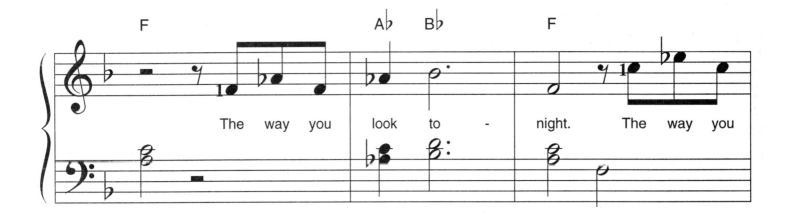

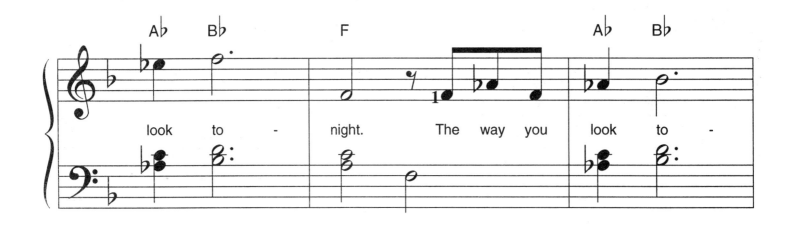

Something About The Way You Look Tonight - 6 - 5

Verse 2:
With your smile you pull the deepest secrets from my heart.
In all honesty, I'm speechless and I don't know where to start.
And I can't explain. . .

Something About The Way You Look Tonight - 6 - 6

HOW DO I LIVE

Recorded by LeAnn Rimes

Words and Music by
DIANE WARREN
Arranged by Richard Bradley

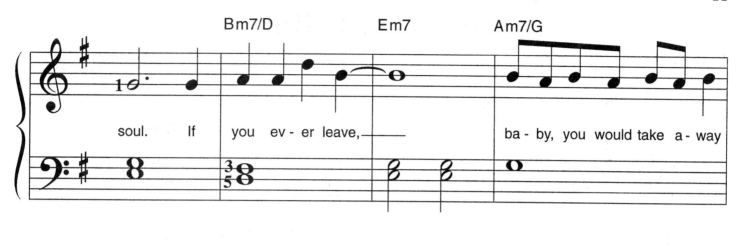

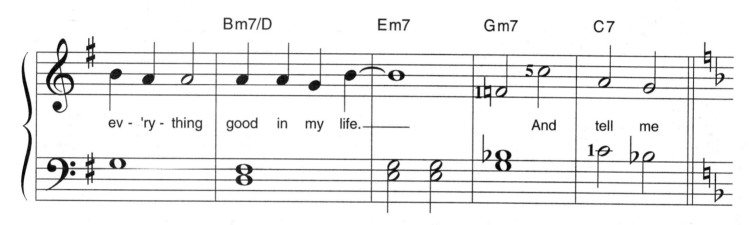

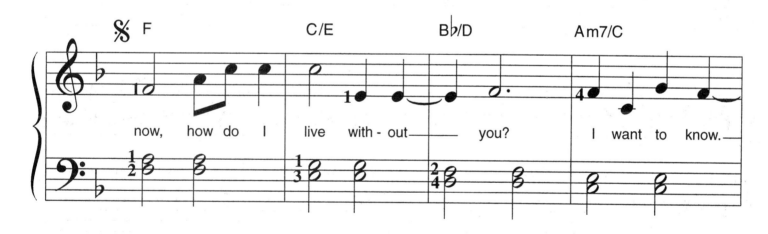

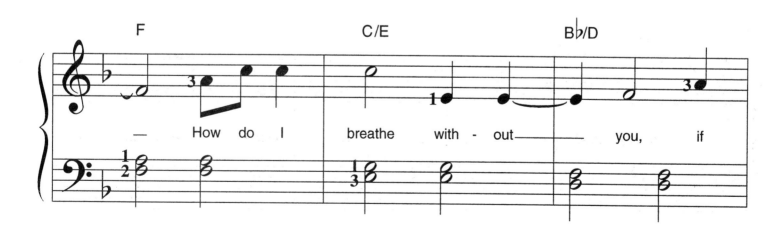

12

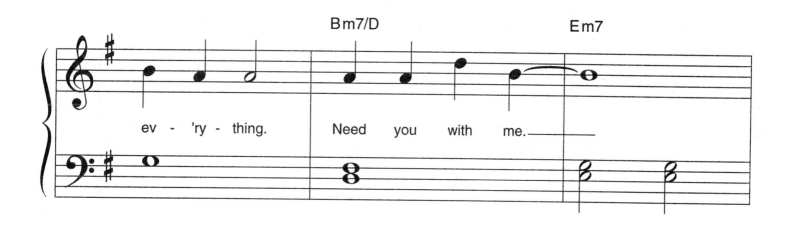

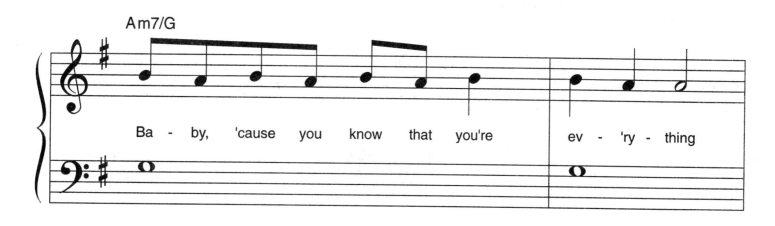

Verse 2:
Without you, there'd be no sun in my sky,
There would be no love in my life,
There'd be no world left for me
And I, baby, I don't know what I would do,
I'd be lost if I lost you.
If you ever leave,
Baby, you would take away everything real in my life,
And tell me now. . .
(To Chorus:).

BUTTERFLY KISSES

Recorded by Bob Carlisle

Words and Music by
BOB CARLISLE and RANDY THOMAS
Arranged by Richard Bradley

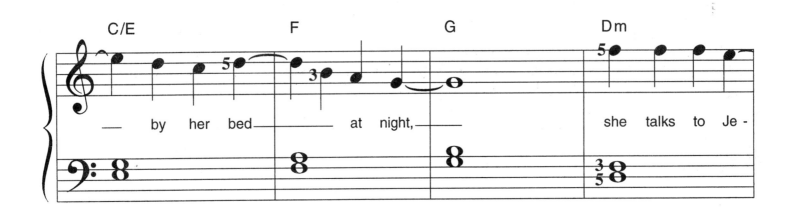

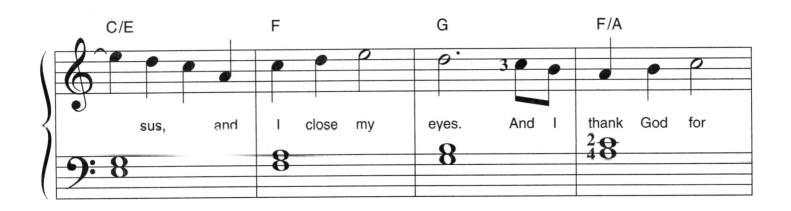

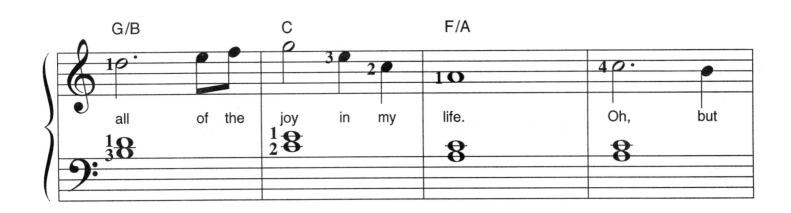

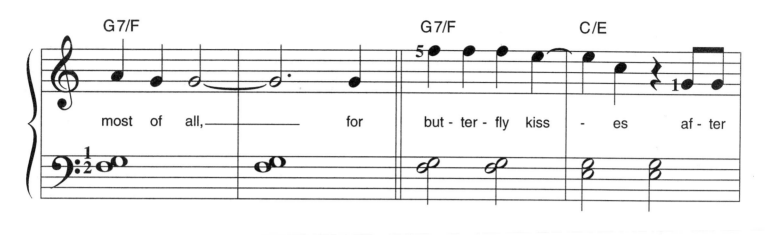

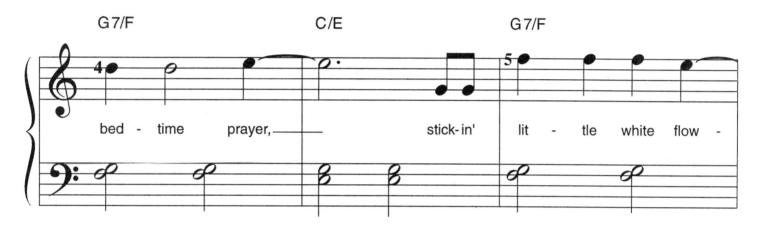

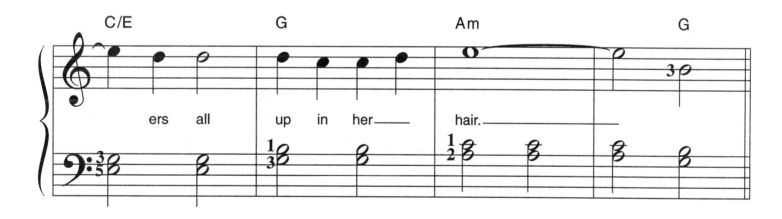

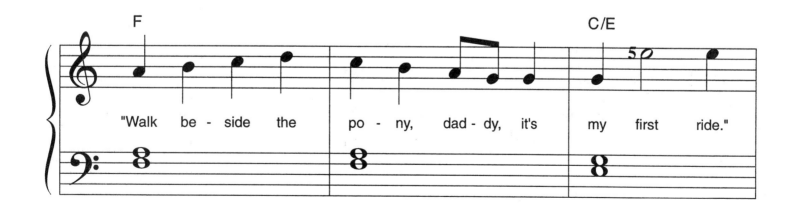

Butterfly Kisses - 7 - 3

18

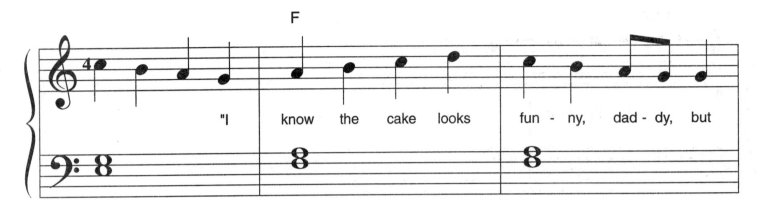

Butterfly Kisses - 7 - 4

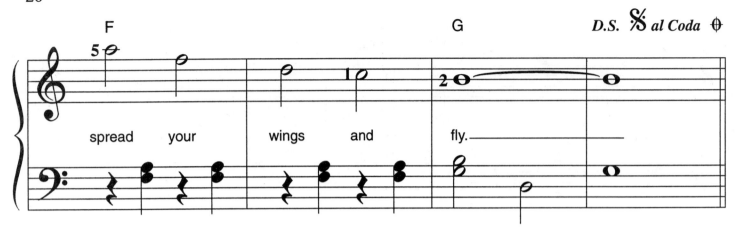

D.S. 𝄋 al Coda ⊕

spread   your   wings   and   fly.

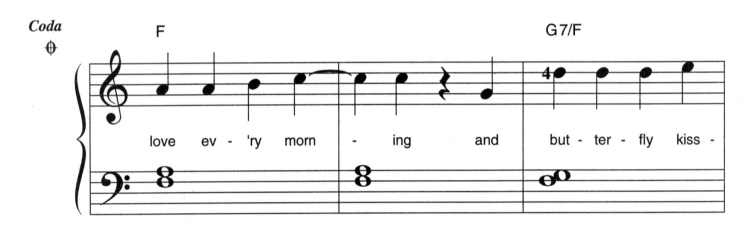

Coda
⊕

love ev - 'ry morn - ing and   but - ter - fly kiss -

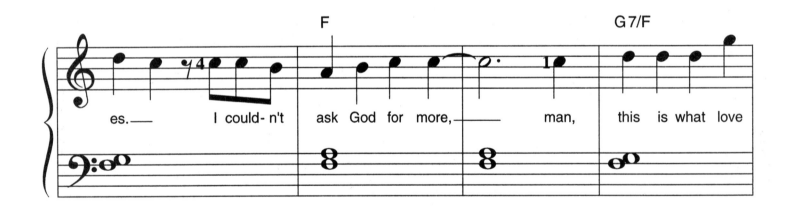

es.___   I could- n't   ask God for more,___   man,   this is what love

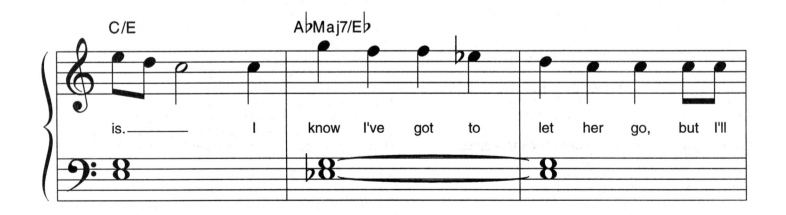

is.___   I   know I've got to   let her go, but I'll

al - ways____ re - mem - ber____ ev - 'ry hug in the morn -

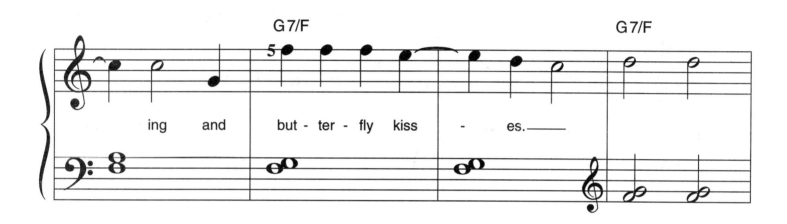

ing and but - ter - fly kiss - es.____

Verse 2:
Sweet sixteen today;
She's looking like her mama a little more ev'ry day.
One part woman, the other part girl;
To perfume and makeup from ribbons and curls;
Trying her wings out in a great big world.
But I remember
Butterfly kisses after bedtime prayer,
Stickin' little white flowers all up in her hair.
"You know how much I love you, daddy,
But if you don't mind,
I'm only gonna kiss you on the cheek this time."
Oh, with all that I've done wrong,
I must have done something right
To deserve her love ev'ry morning
And butterfly kisses at night.
(All the precious time.)
Oh, like the wind, the years go by.
(Precious butterfly, spread your wings and fly.)

Verse 3:
She'll change her name today.
She'll make a promise, and I'll give her away.
Standing in the bride room just staring at her,
She asks me what I'm thinking,
And I say, "I'm not sure.
I just feel like I'm losing my baby girl."
Then she leaned over and gave me
Butterfly kisses with her mama there,
Stickin' little white flowers all up in her hair.
"Walk me down the aisle, daddy, it's just about time."
"Does my wedding gown look pretty, daddy?"
"Daddy, don't cry."
Oh, with all that I've done wrong,
I must have done something right
To deserve her love ev'ry morning and butterfly kisses.
I couldn't ask God for more,
Man, this is what love is.
I know I've got to let her go, but I'll always remember
Ev'ry hug in the morning and butterfly kisses.

Butterfly Kisses - 7 - 7

QUIT PLAYING GAMES
(WITH MY HEART)

Recorded by Backstreet Boys

Words and Music by
MAX MARTIN and HERBERT CRICHLOW
Arranged by Richard Bradley

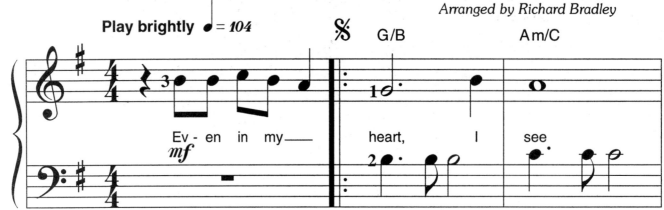

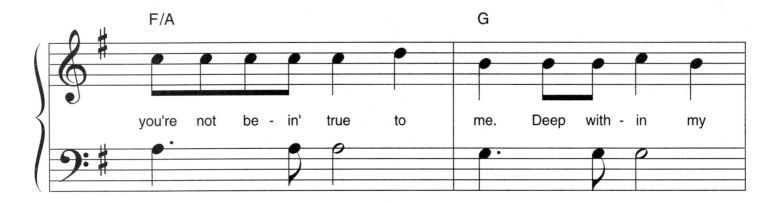

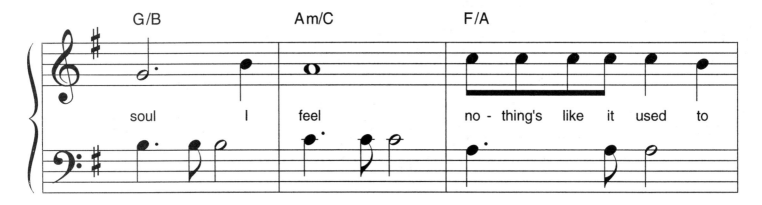

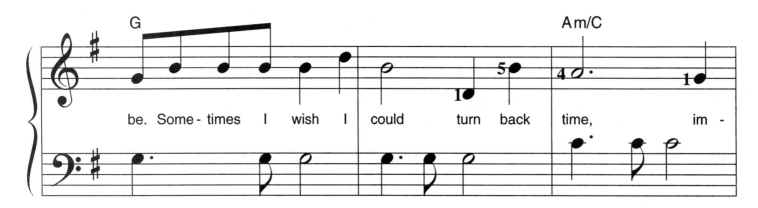

Quit Playing Games - 4 - 1

23

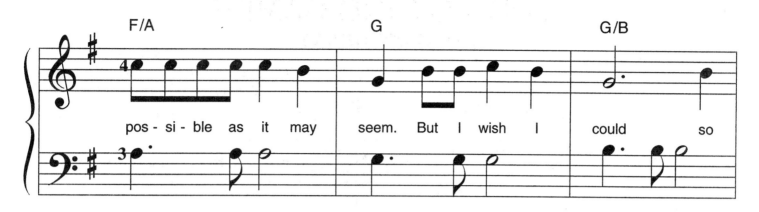

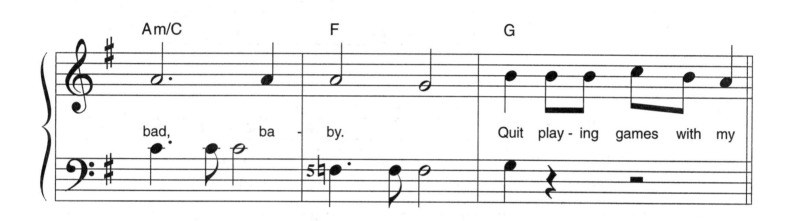

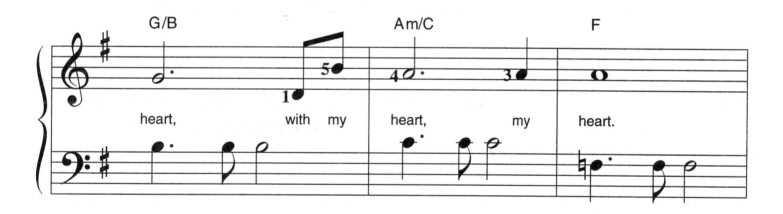

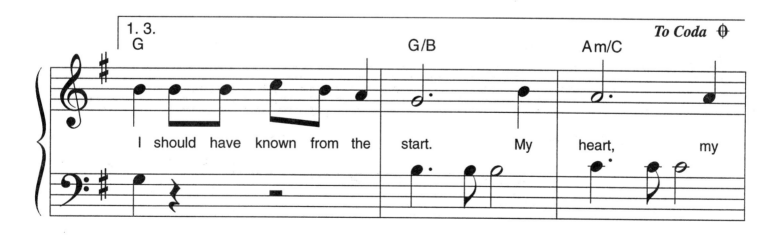

Quit Playing Games - 4 - 2

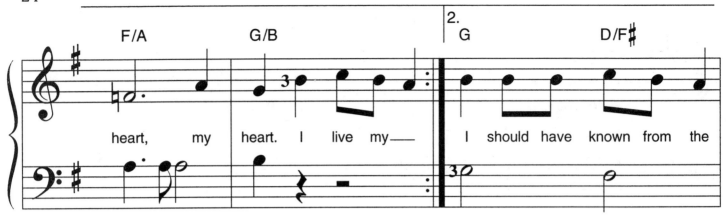

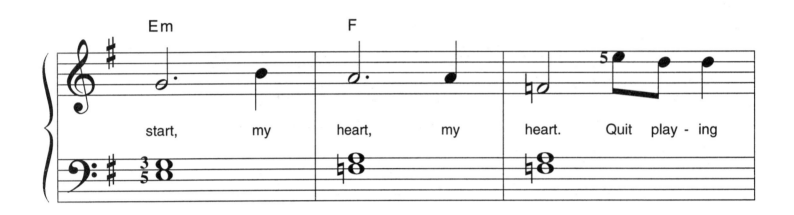

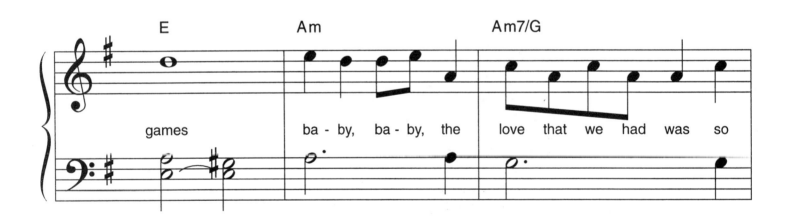

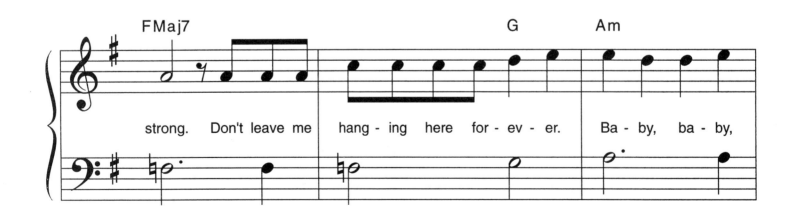

this is not a lie, let's | stop this to - night._____ | *3rd verse instrumental*

Coda
⊕

heart. | Quit play - ing games with my | heart.

Verse 2:
I live my life the way,
To keep you coming back to me.
Everything I do is for you,
So what is it that you can't see?
Sometimes I wish I could turn back time,
Impossible as it may seem.
But I wish I could so bad, baby
You better quit playing games with my heart.

AT THE BEGINNING

From the Twentieth Century Fox Motion Picture "Anastasia"
Recorded by Richard Marx and Donna Lewis

Lyrics by LYNN AHRENS
Music by STEPHRN FLAHERTY
Arranged by Richard Bradley

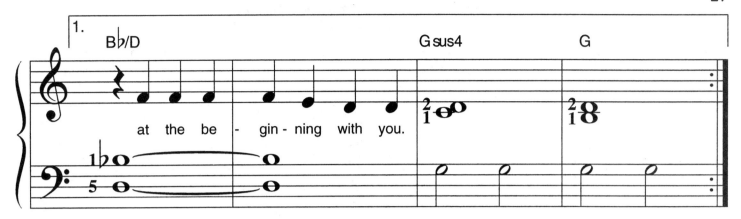

1. at the be - gin - ning with you.

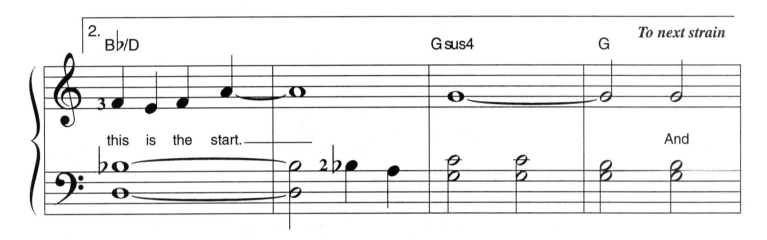

2. this is the start. And

To next strain

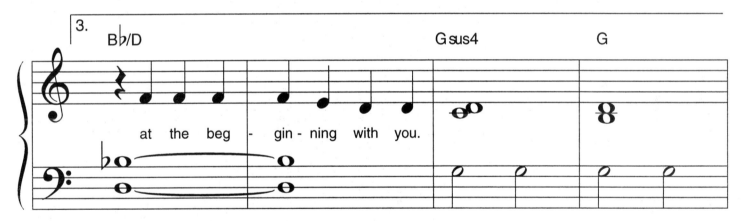

3. at the beg - gin - ning with you.

mf life is a road, and I want to keep go - ing. Love is a riv - er, I wan -

28

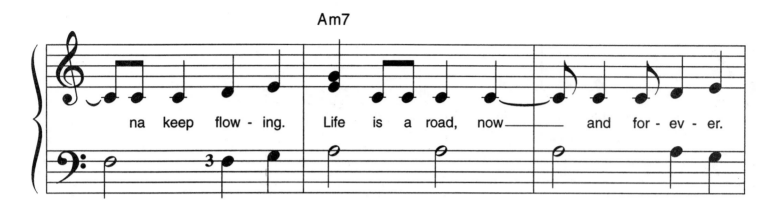

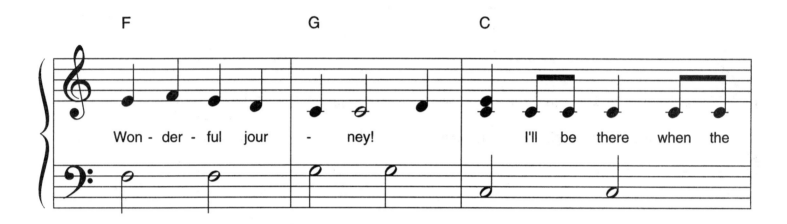

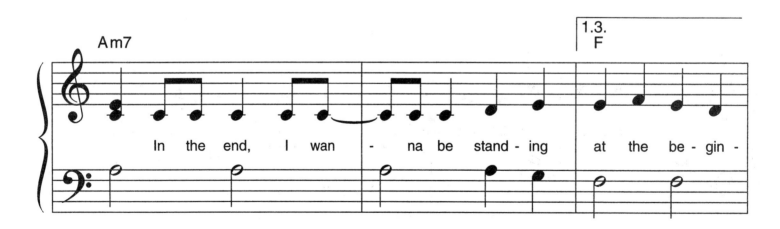

At The Beginning - 5 - 3

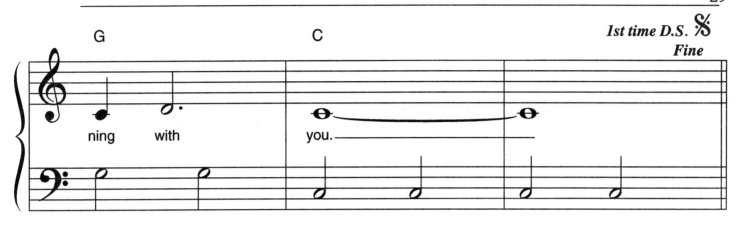

ning with   you._____

2.

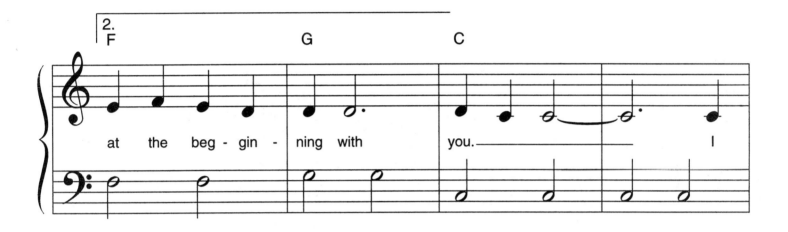

at   the   beg - gin - ning   with   you._____   I

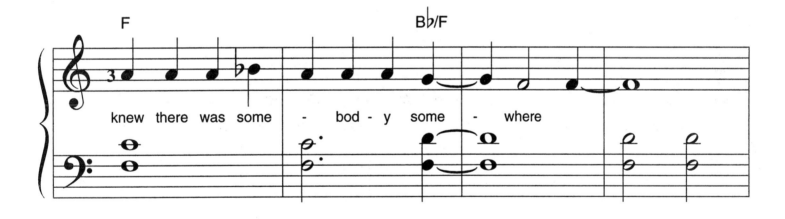

knew there was some - bod - y some - where

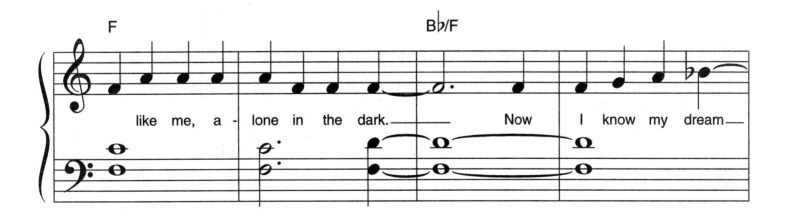

like me, a - lone in the dark._____   Now   I know my dream_____

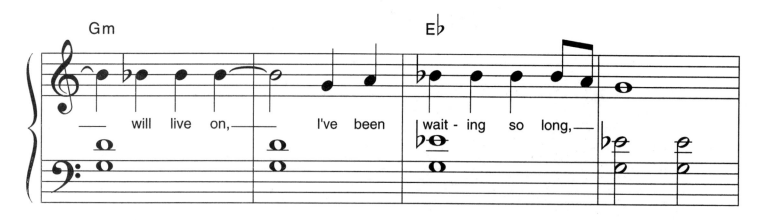

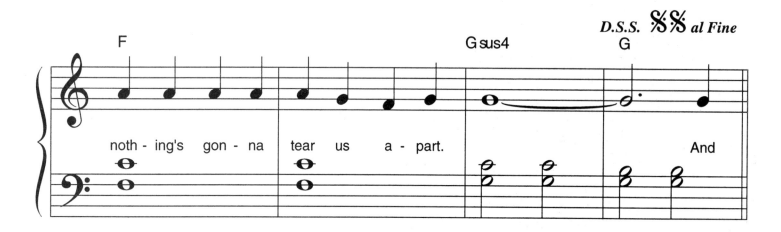

Verse 2:
No one told me I was going to find you.
Unexpected, what you did to my heart.
When I lost hope,
You were there to remind me this is the start.

Verse 3:
We were strangers on a crazy adventure
Never dreaming how our dreams would come true.
Now here we stand, unafraid of the future,
At the beginning with you.

FOR YOU I WILL

Recorded by Monica

Words and Music by
DIANE WARREN
Arranged by Richard Bradley

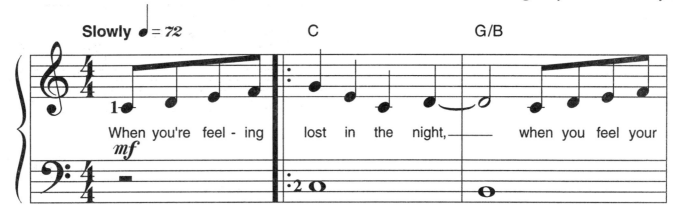

When you're feel-ing lost in the night,—— when you feel your

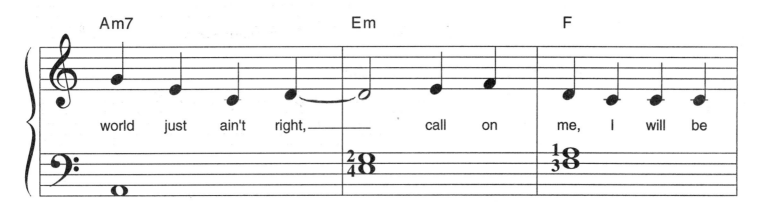

world just ain't right,—— call on me, I will be

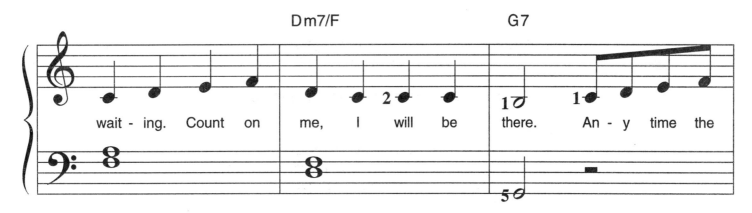

wait-ing. Count on me, I will be there. An-y time the

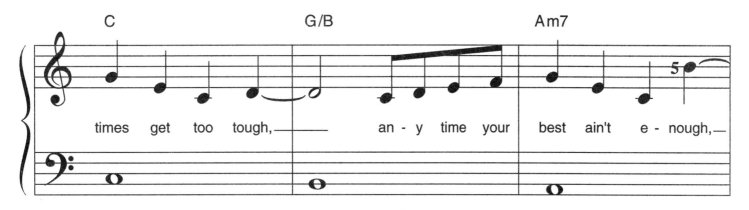

times get too tough,—— an-y time your best ain't e-nough,——

For You I Will - 5 - 1

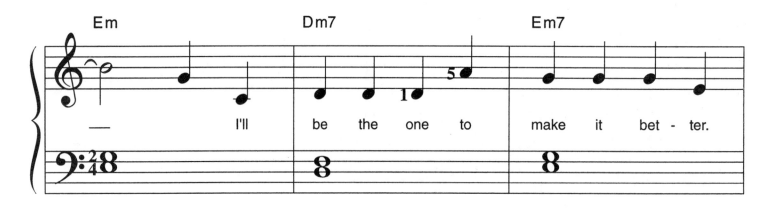

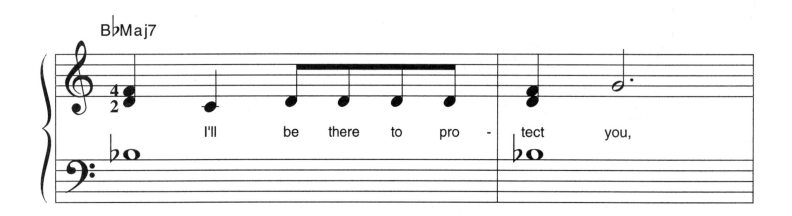

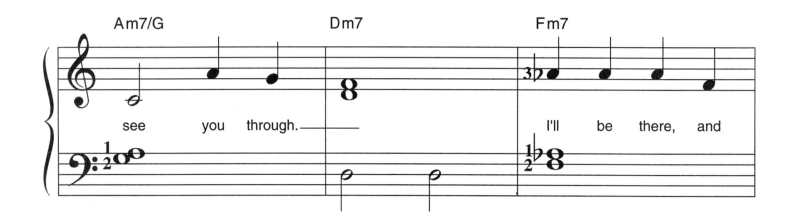

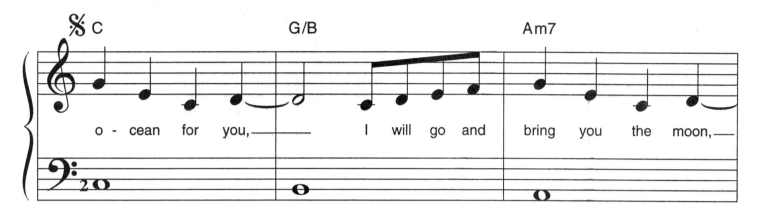

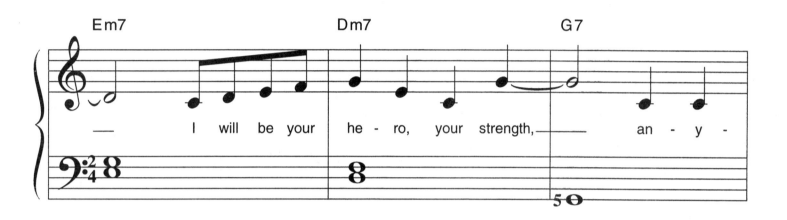

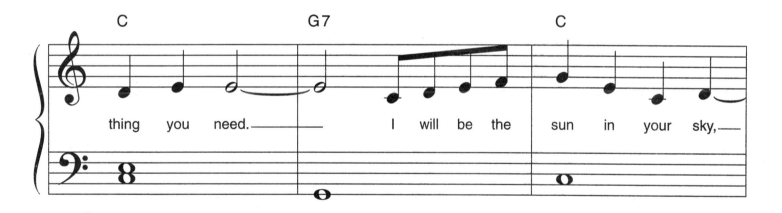

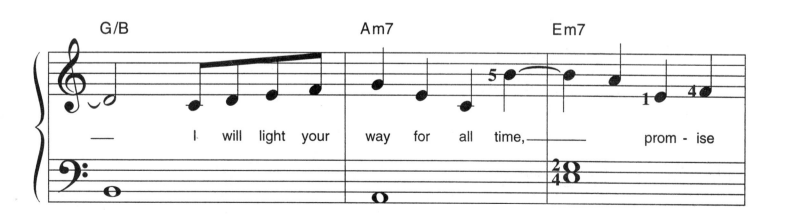

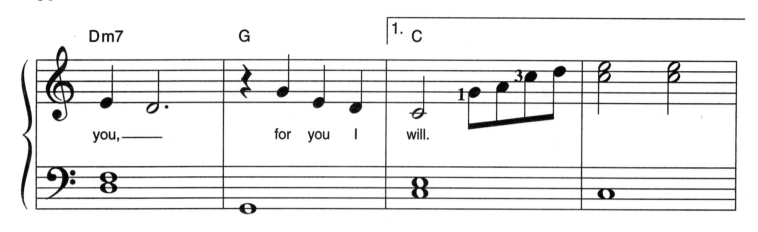

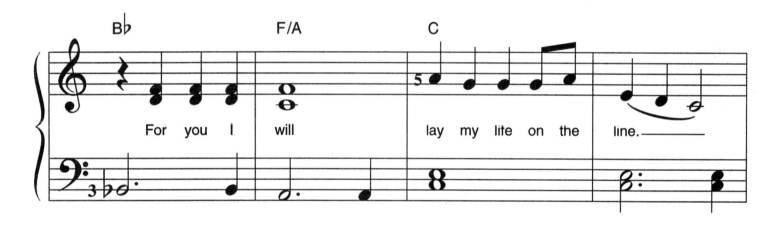

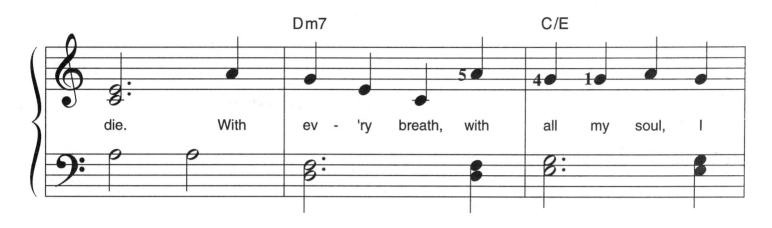

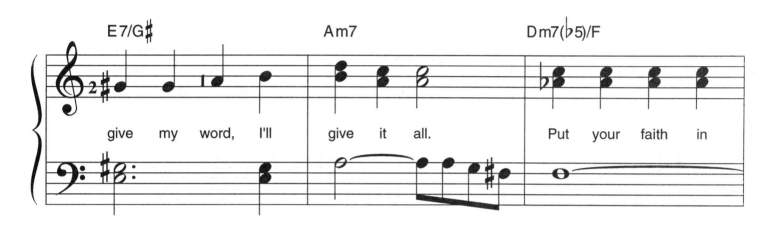

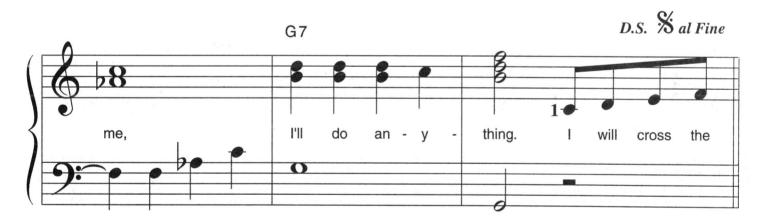

Verse 2:
I will shield your heart from the rain,
I won't let no harm come your way.
Oh, these arms will be your shelter,
No, these arms won't let you down.
If there is a mountain to move,
I will move that mountain for you.
I'm here for you, I'm here forever.
I will be a fortress, tall and strong.
I'll keep you safe, I'll stand beside you,
Right or wrong.

SAY YOU'LL BE THERE

Recorded by Spice Girls

Words and Music by
SPICE GIRLS
and ELIOT KENNEDY
Arranged by Richard Bradley

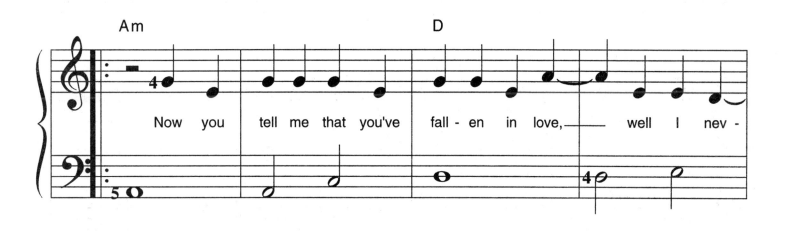

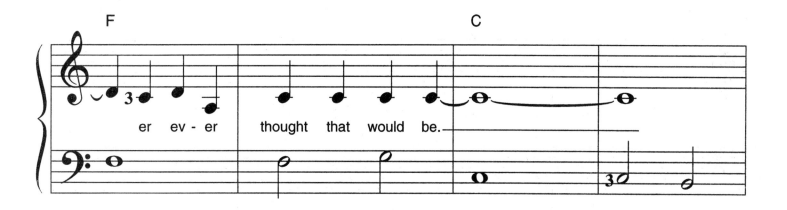

Say You'll Be There - 6 - 2

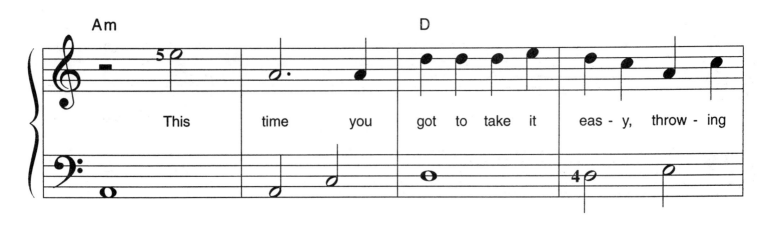

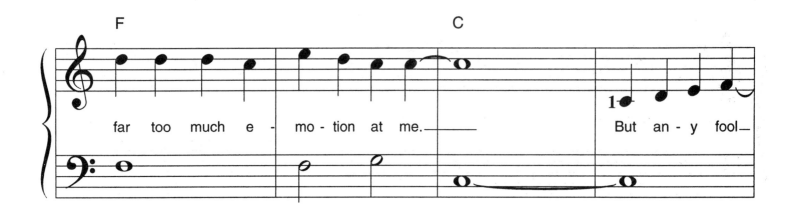

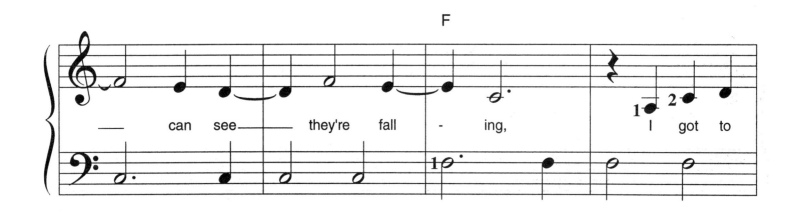

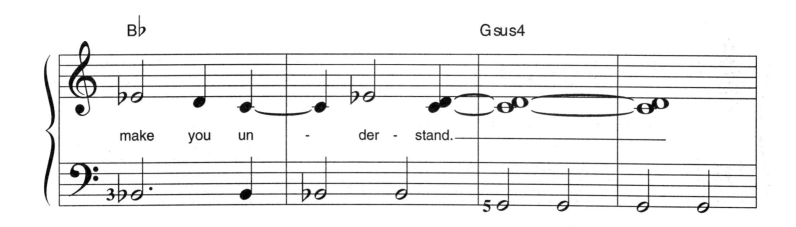

40

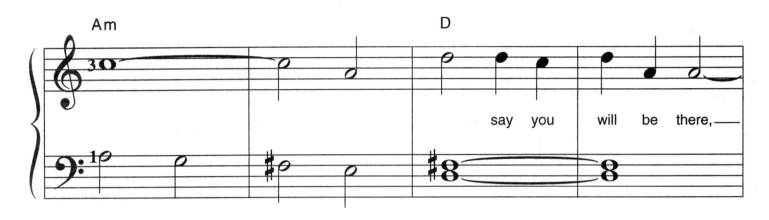

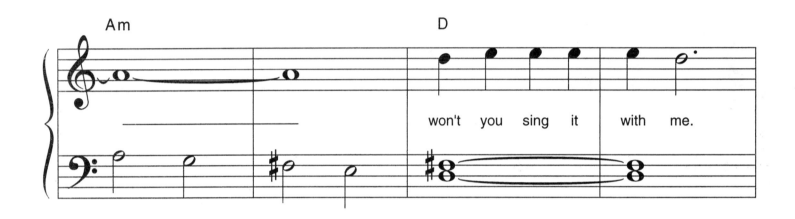

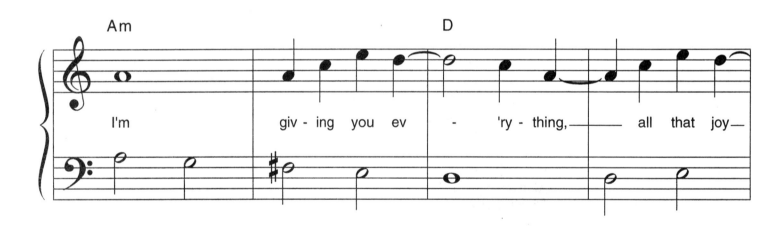

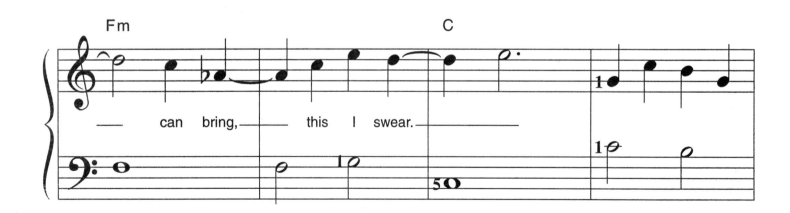

Say You'll Be There - 6 - 5

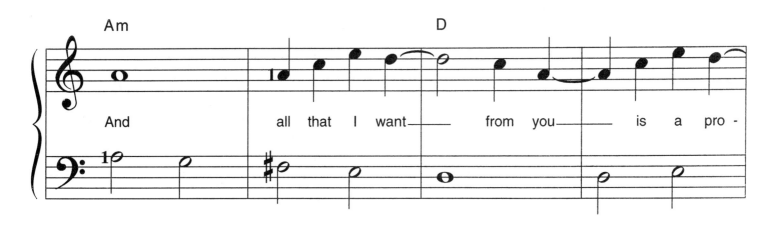

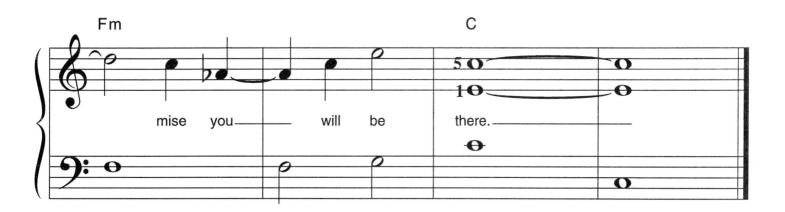

Verse 2:
If you put two and two together,
You will see what our friendship is for.
If you can't work out the equation
Then I guess I'll have to show you the door.
There is no need to say you love me,
It would be better left unsaid.

I'm giving you everything,
All that joy can bring,
This I swear.
And all that I want from you
Is a promise you will be there.

YOU WERE MEANT FOR ME

Recorded by Jewel

Words and Music by
JEWEL KILCHER and STEVE POLTZ
Arranged by Richard Bradley

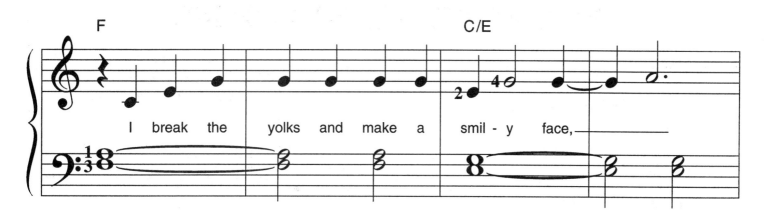

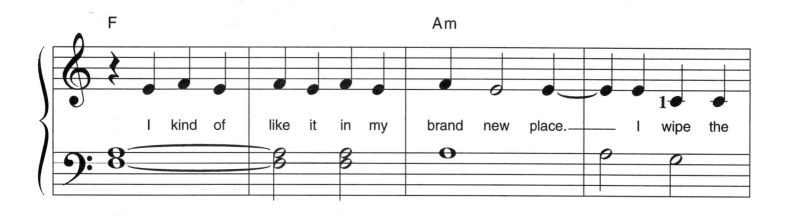

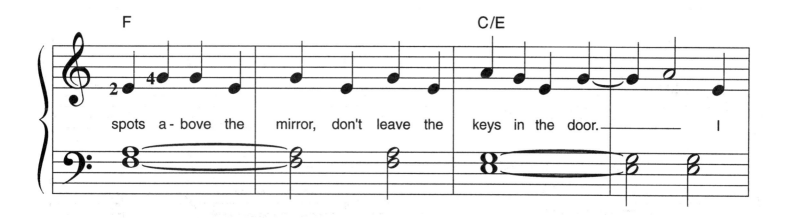

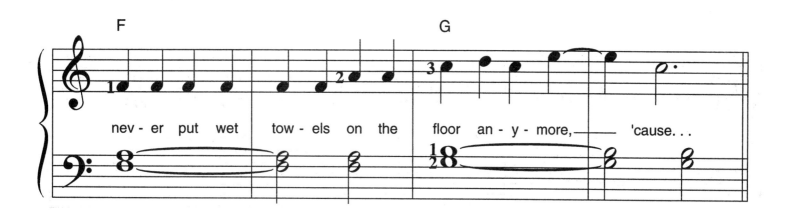

You Were Meant For Me - 6 - 2

44

Chorus:

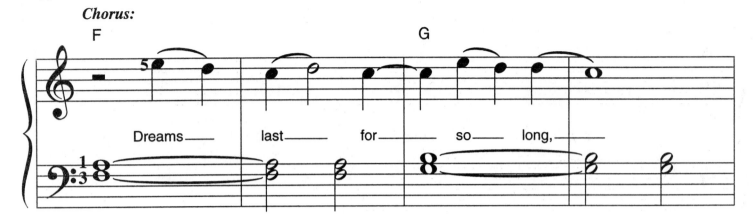

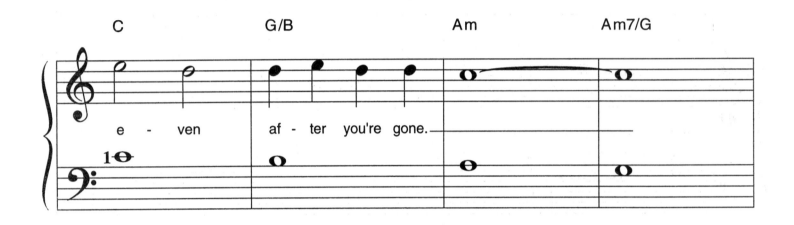

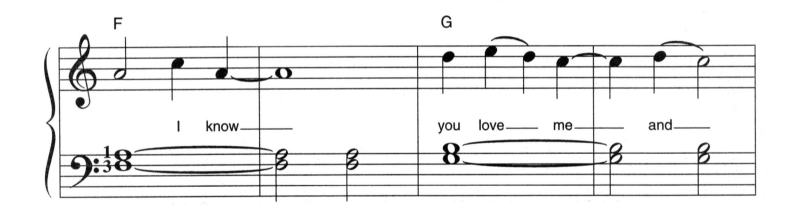

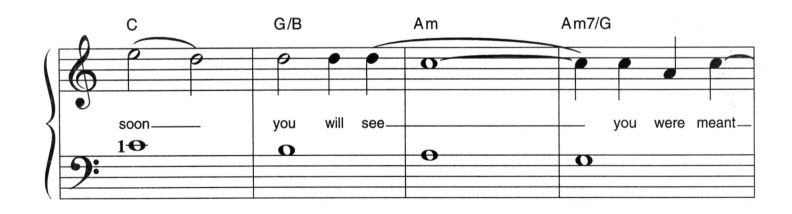

You Were Meant For Me - 6 - 3

F

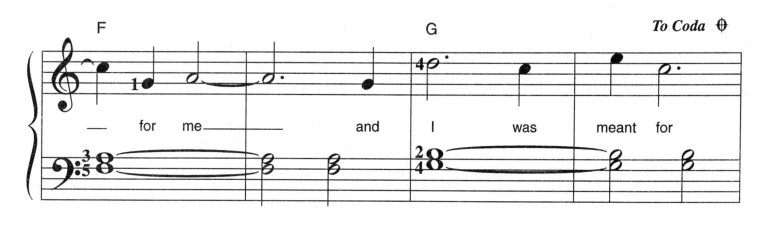

for me _____ and I was meant for

1. Am

you. _____

2. Am

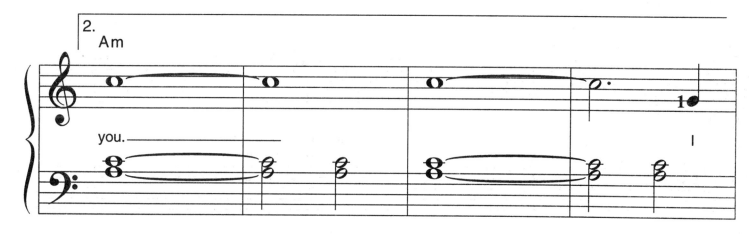

you. _____ I

Dm7   G

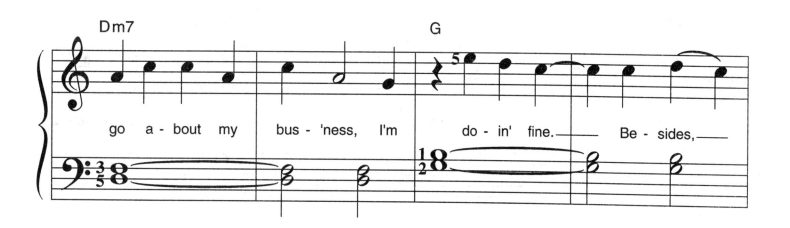

go a - bout my bus - 'ness, I'm doin' fine. ____ Be - sides, ____

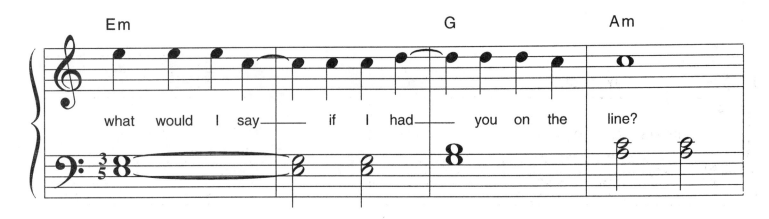

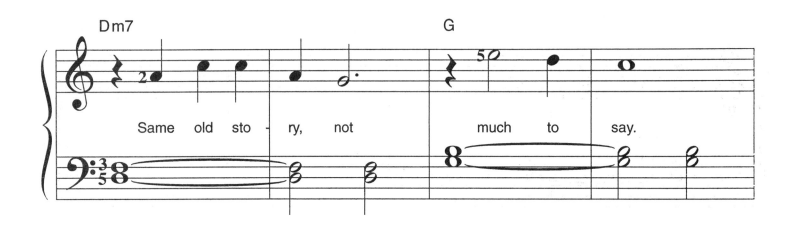

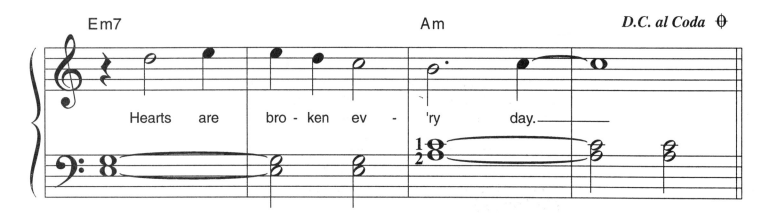

Coda

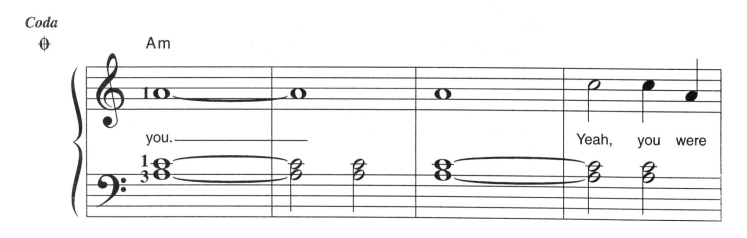

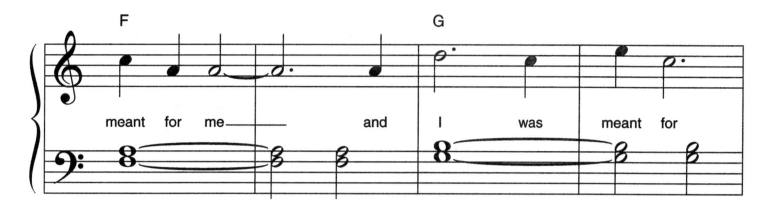

meant for me_____ and I was meant for

you.____

Verse 2:
I called my mama, she was out for a walk.
Consoled a cup of coffee, but it didn't wanna talk.
So I picked up a paper, it was more bad news,
More hearts being broken or people being used.
Put on my coat in the pouring rain.
I saw a movie, it just wasn't the same,
'Cause it was happy and I was sad,
And it made me miss you, oh, so bad.
(To Chorus:)

Verse 3:
I brush my teeth and put the cap back on,
I know you hate it when I leave the light on.
I pick a book up and then turn the sheets down,
And then I take a breath and a good look around.
Put on my pj's and hop into bed.
I'm half alive but I feel mostly dead.
I try and tell myself it'll be all right,
I just shouldn't think anymore tonight.
(To Chorus:)

HARD TO SAY I'M SORRY

Recorded by Az Yet Featuring Peter Cetera

Words and Music by
DAVID FOSTER and PETER CETERA
Arranged by Richard Bradley

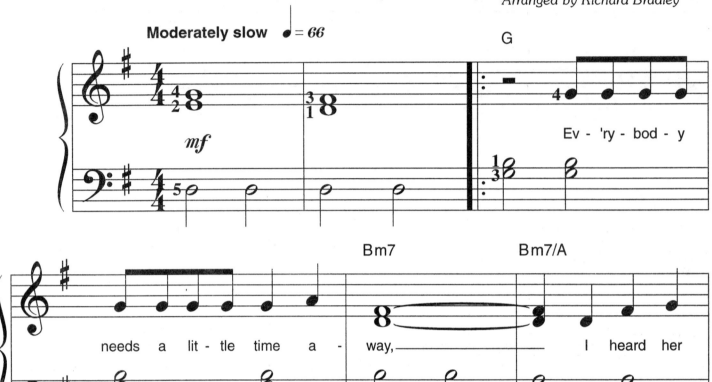

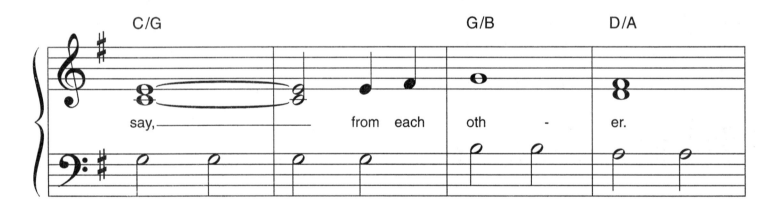

Hard To Say I'm Sorry - 4 - 1

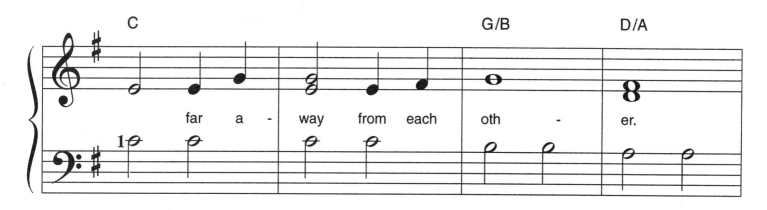

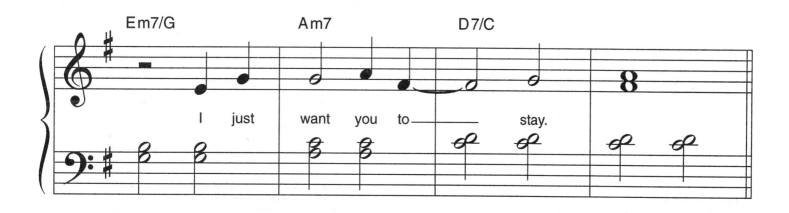

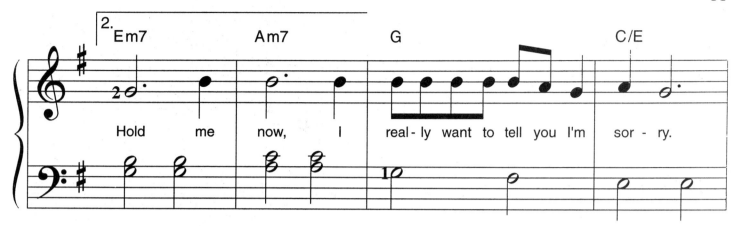

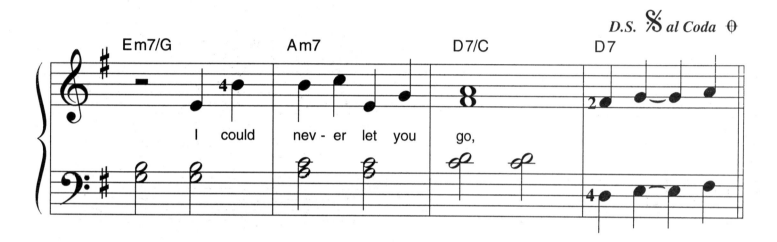

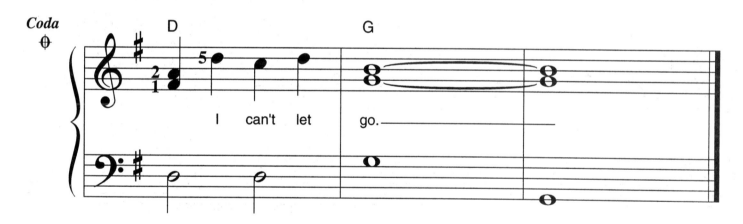

Verse 2:
Couldn't stand to be kept away,
Not for a day, from your body.
Wouldn't wanna be swept away,
Far away from the one that I love.
Hold me now,
It's hard for me to say I'm sorry.
I just want you to know.

BECAUSE YOU LOVED ME
(THEME FROM "UP CLOSE & PERSONAL")

Recorded by Celiene Dion

Words and Music by
DIANE WARREN
Arranged by Richard Bradley

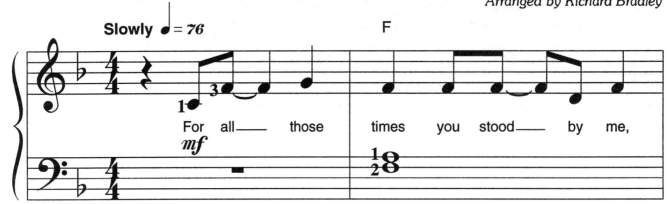

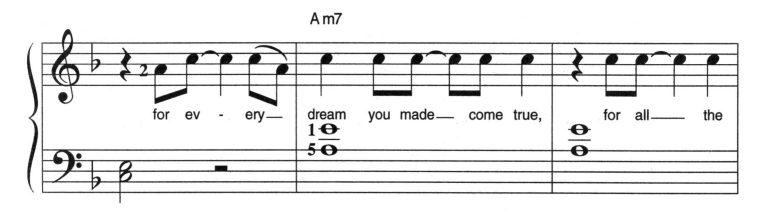

Because You Loved Me - 5 - 1

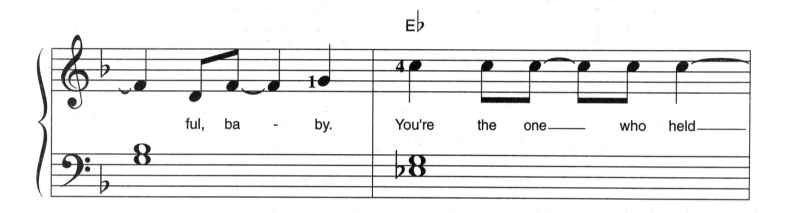

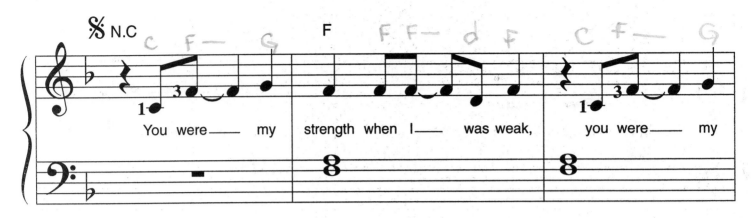

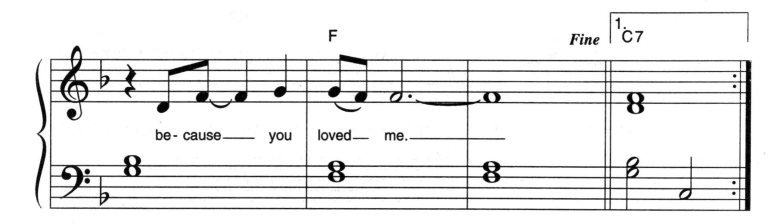

Because You Loved Me - 5 - 4

56

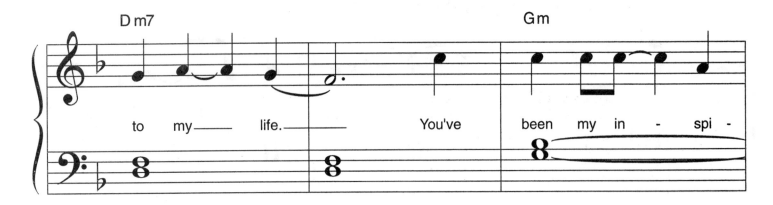

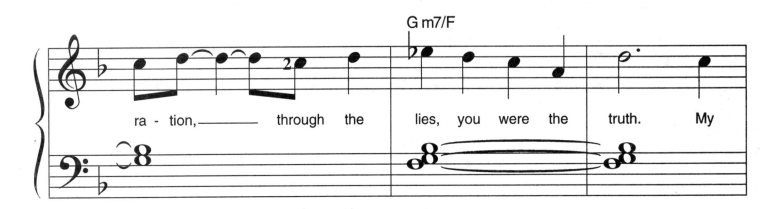

Verse 2:
You gave me wings and made me fly,
You touched my hand, I could touch the sky.
I lost my faith you gave it back to me.
You said no star was out of reach,
You stood by me and I stood tall.
I had your love, I had it all.
I'm grateful for each day you gave me.
Maybe I don't know that much,
But I know this much is true.
I was blessed because I was loved by you.

FOLLOW YOU DOWN

Recorded by Gin Blossoms

Words and Music by
D. SCOTT JOHNSON, BILL LEEN, PHIL RHODES,
JESSE VALENZUELA and ROBIN WILSON
Arranged by Richard Bradley

Moderately fast ♩ = 128

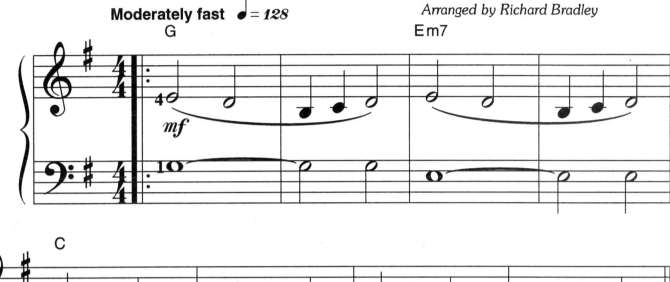

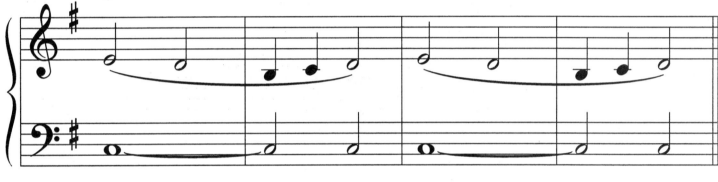

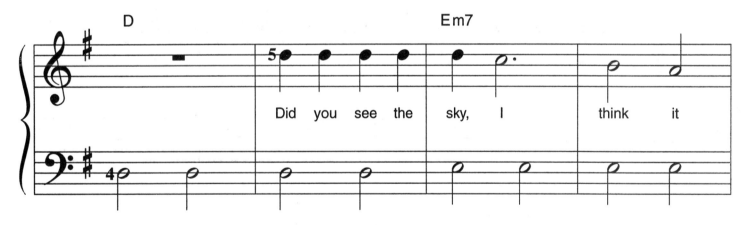

Did you see the sky, I think it

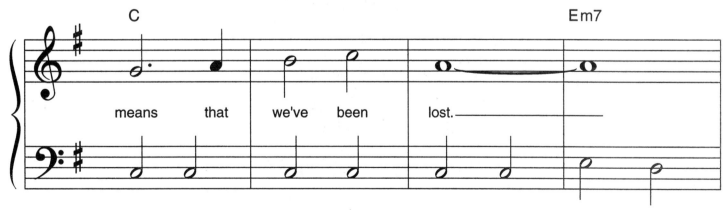

means that we've been lost.

Follow You Down - 5 - 1

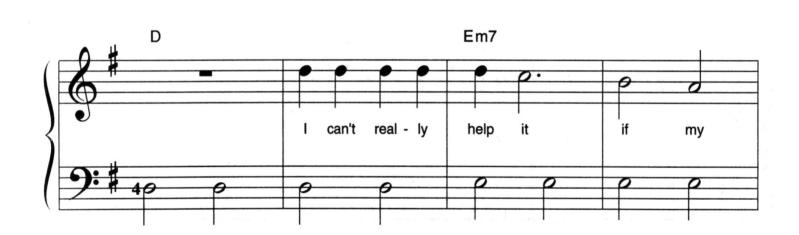

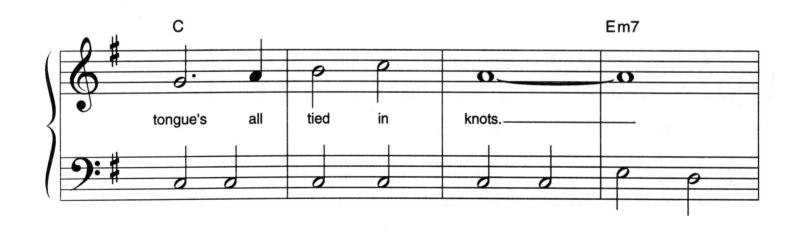

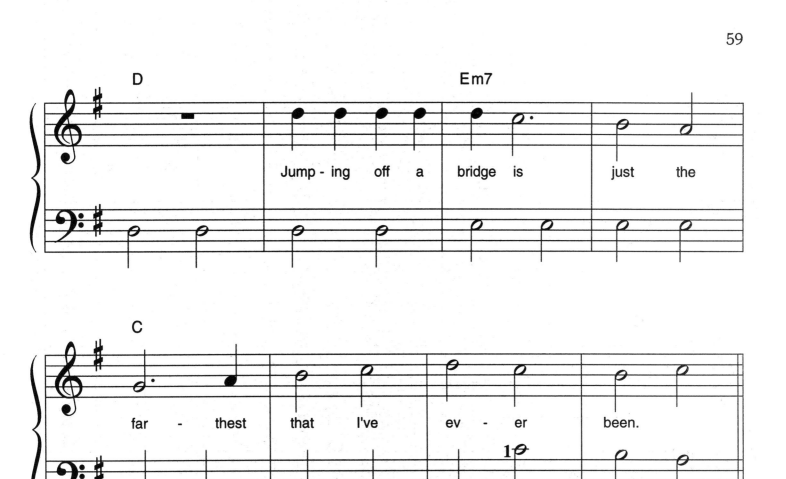

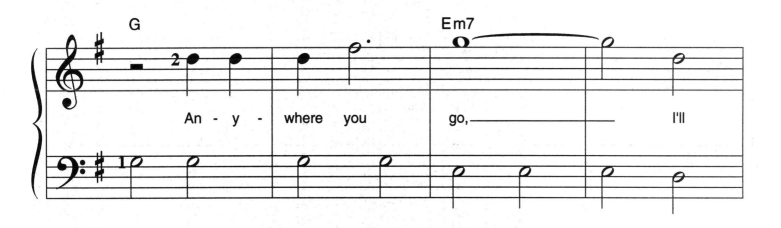

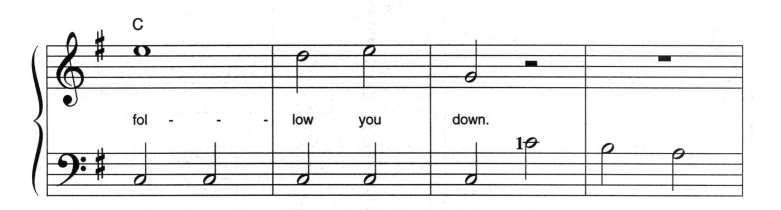

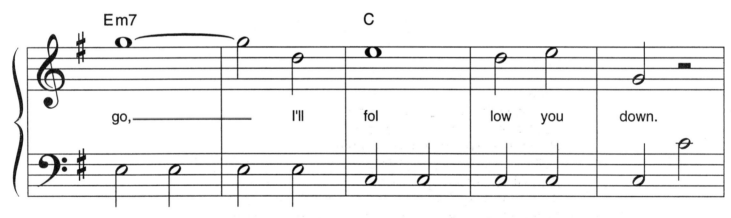

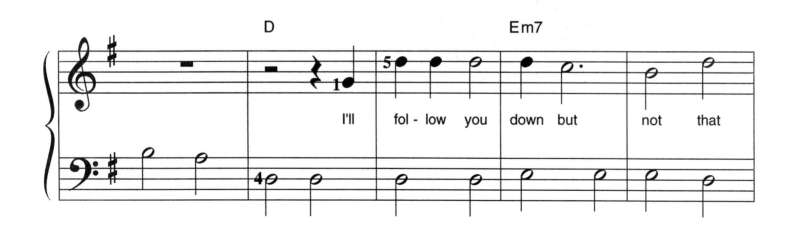

Verse 2:
I know we're headed somewhere,
I can see how far we've come.
But still I can't remember anything.
Let's not do the wrong thing
And I'll swear it might be fun.
It's a long way down
When all the knots we're tied have come undone.

Verse 3:
How you gonna ever find your place
Running at an artificial pace?
Are they gonna find us lying face down in the sand?
So what, now, we've already been forever damned.

I LOVE YOU ALWAYS FOREVER

Recorded by Donna Lewis

Words and Music by
DONNA LEWIS
Arranged by Richard Bradley

63

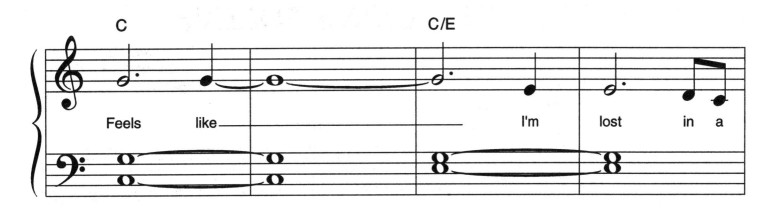

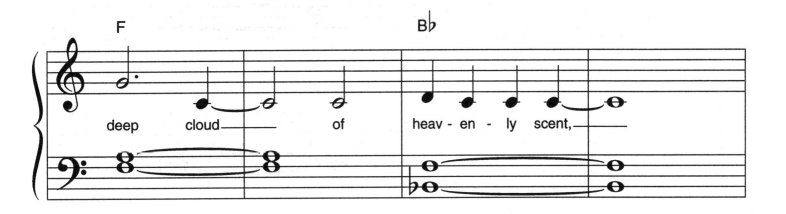

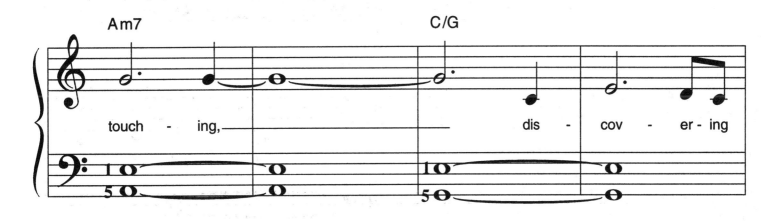

I Love You Always Forever - 6 - 2

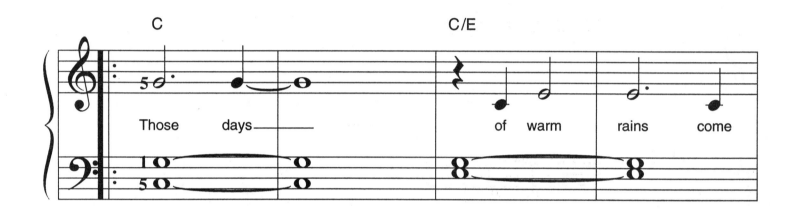

Those days⎯⎯⎯⎯ of warm rains come

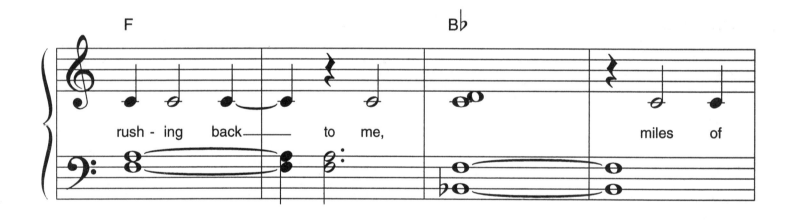

rush - ing back⎯⎯ to me, miles of

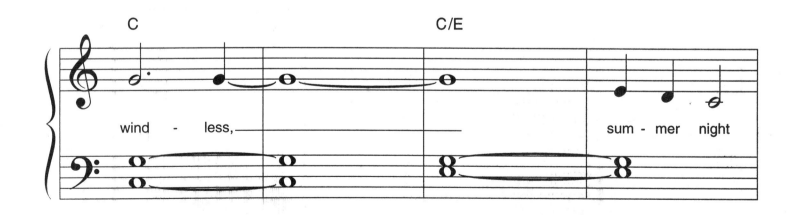

wind - less,⎯⎯⎯⎯⎯⎯⎯⎯⎯ sum - mer night

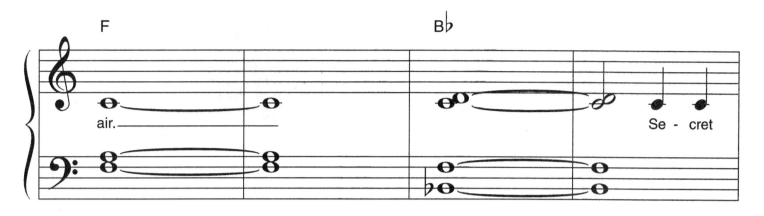

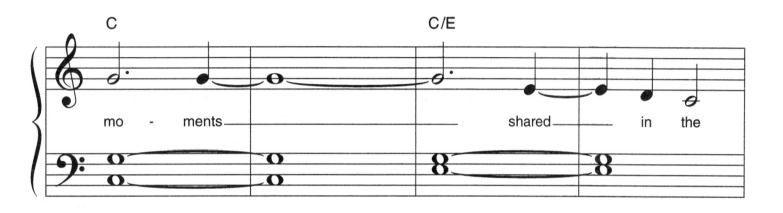

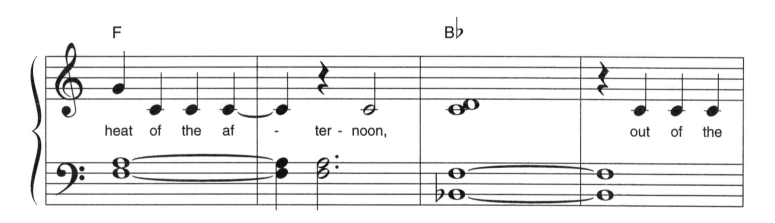

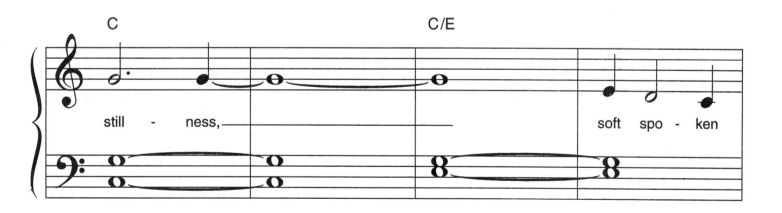

66

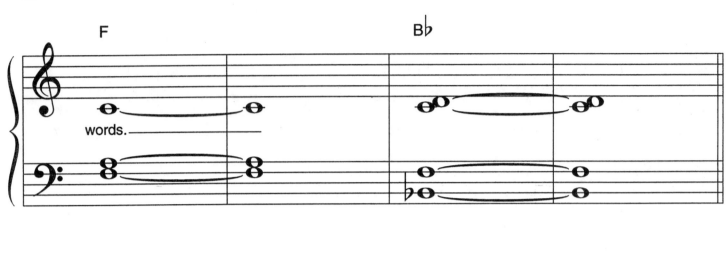

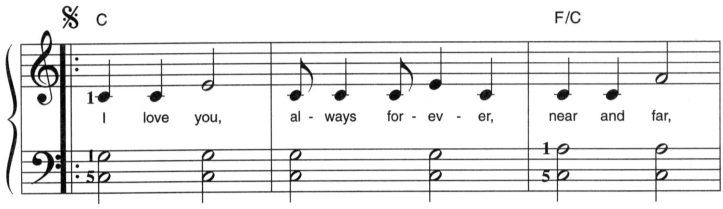

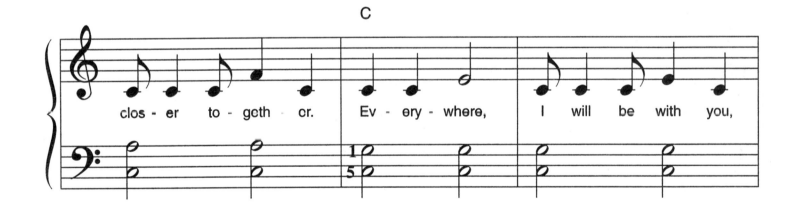

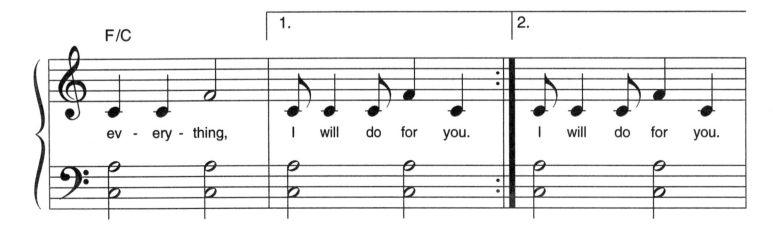

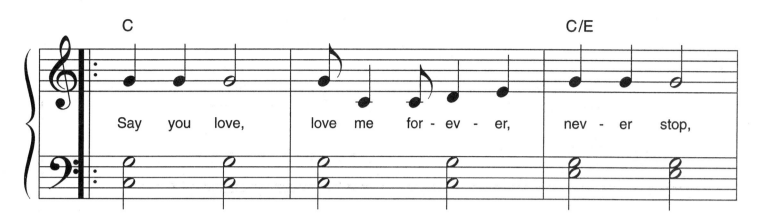

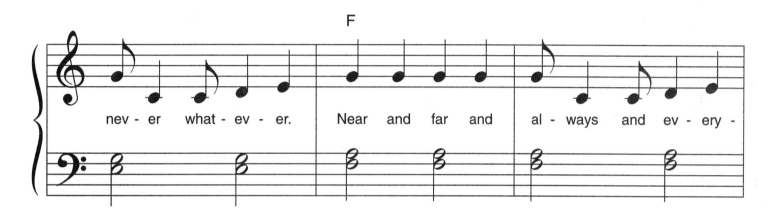

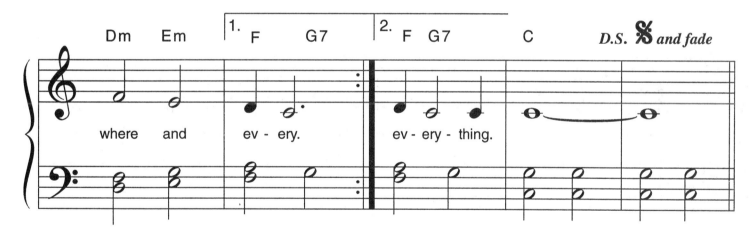

Verse 3:
You've got the most unbelievable blue eyes I've ever seen.
You've got me almost melting away as we lay there
Under blue sky with pure white stars,
Exotic sweetness, a magical time,
(To Chorus:)

UN–BREAK MY HEART

Recorded by Toni Braxton

Words and Music by
DIANE WARREN
Arranged by Richard Bradley

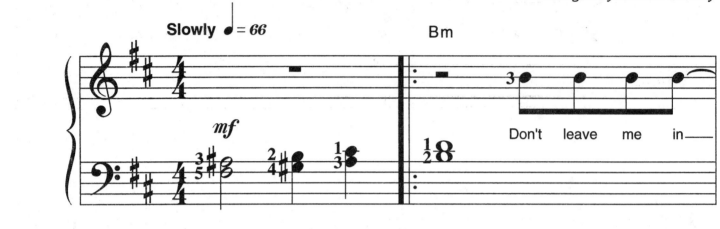

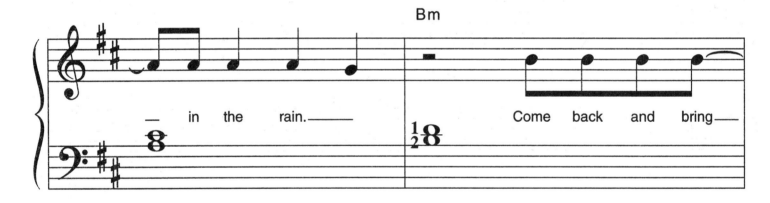

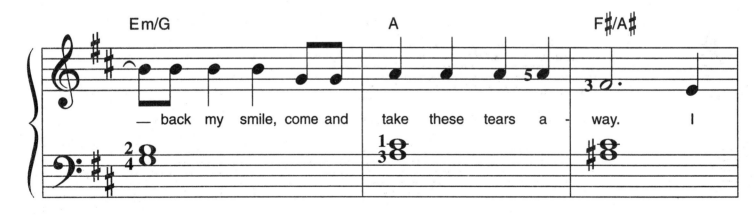

Un-Break My Heart - 4 - 1

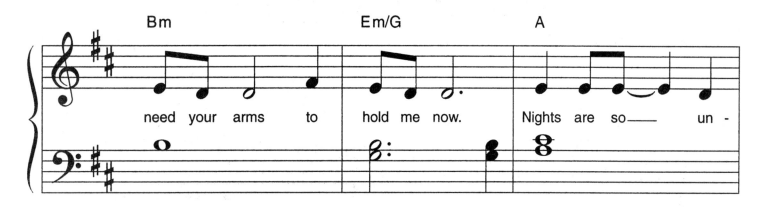

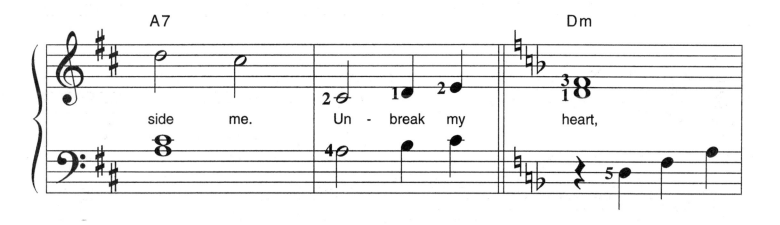

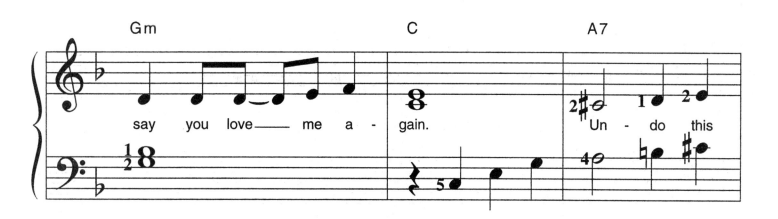

Un-Break My Heart - 4 - 2

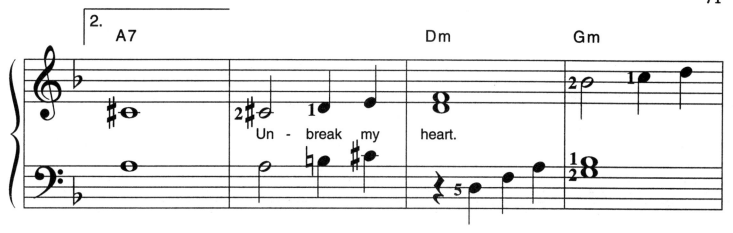

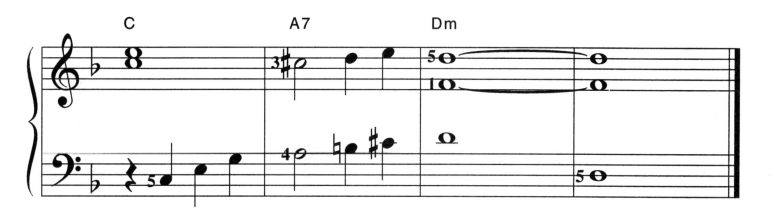

Verse 2:
Take back that sad word goodbye,
Bring back the joy to my life.
Don't leave me here with these tears,
Come and kiss this pain away.
I can't forget the day you left.
Time is so unkind,
And life is so cruel without you here beside me.

YOU LIGHT UP MY LIFE

Recorded by LeAnn Rimes

Words and Music by
JOE BROOKS
Arranged by Richard Bradley

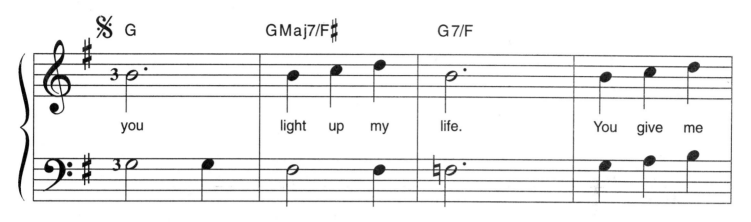

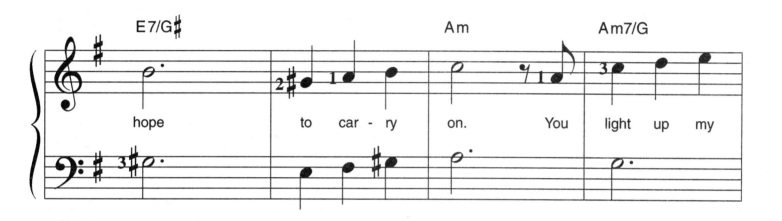

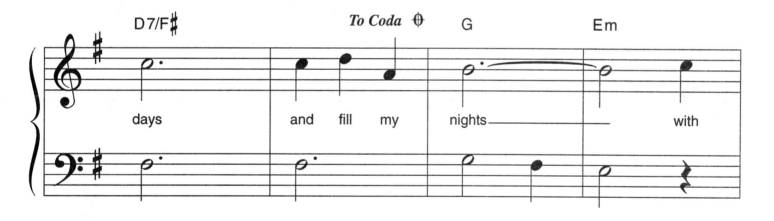

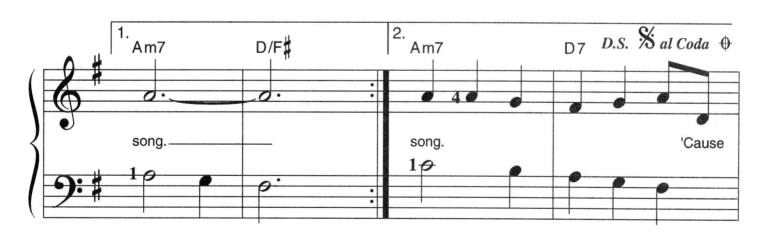

74

Coda

Verse 2:
Rollin' at sea, a drift on the waters,
Could it be fin'lly I'm turning for home?
Fin'lly a chance to say,"Hey! I love you."
Never again to be all alone.

I BELIEVE IN YOU AND ME

From the Motion Picture "The Preacher's Wife"
Recorded by Whitney Houston

Words and Music by
SANDY LINZER and DAVID WOLFERT
Arranged by Richard Bradley

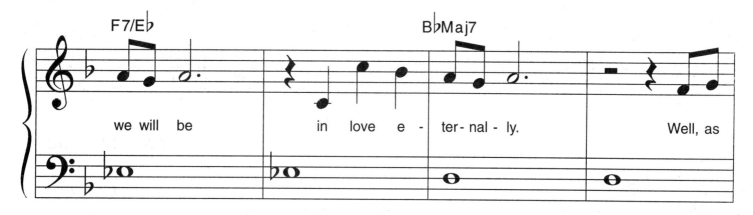

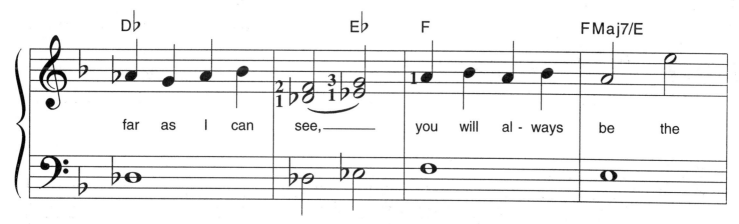

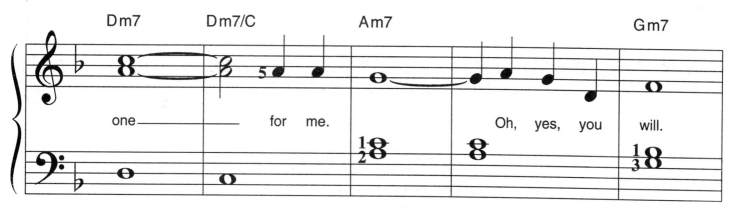

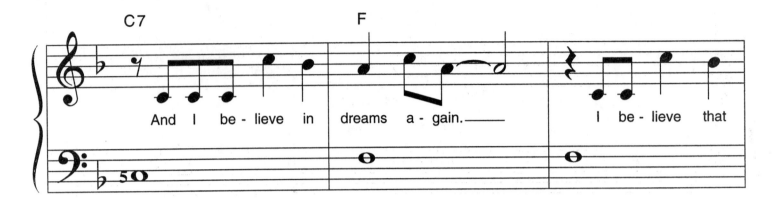

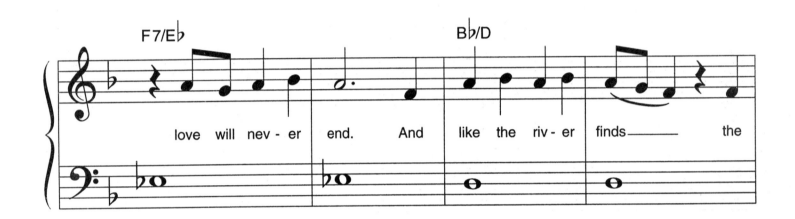

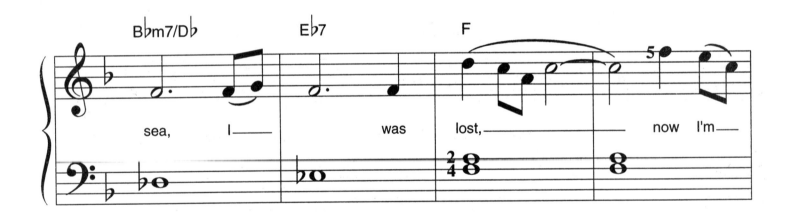

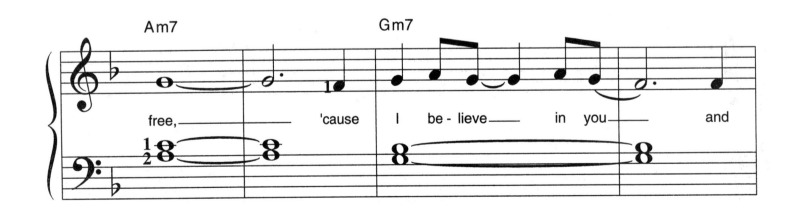

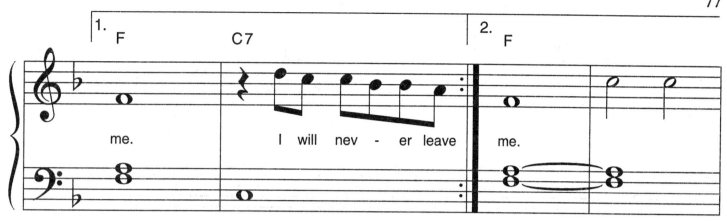

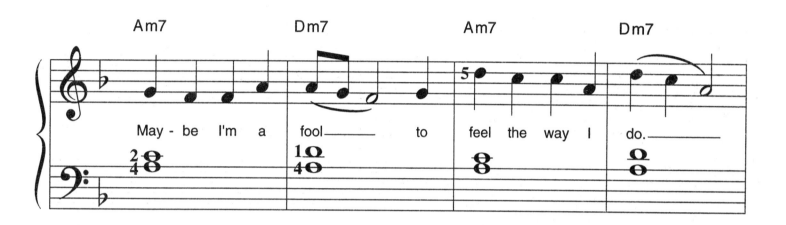

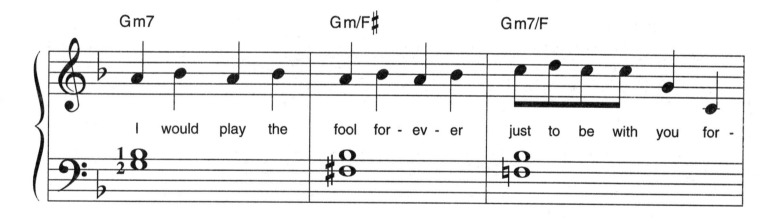

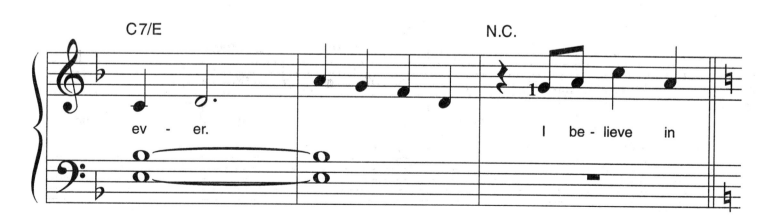

I Believe In You And Me - 5 - 3

78

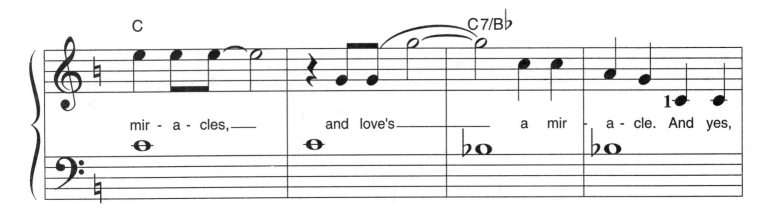

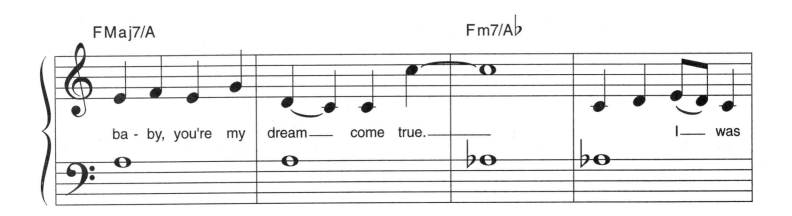

I Believe In You And Me - 5 - 4

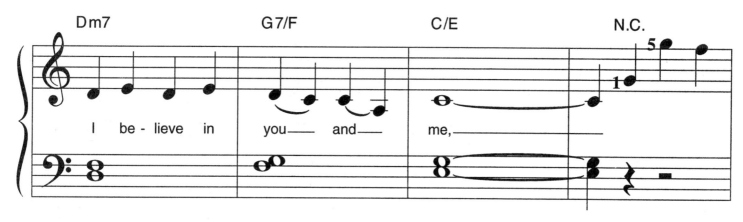

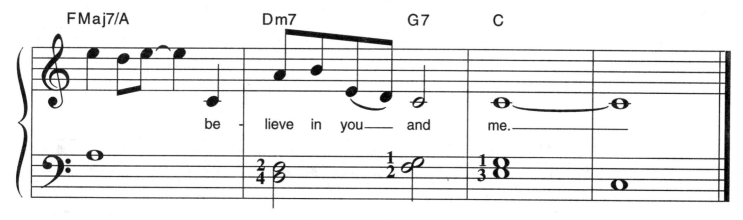

Verse 2:
I will never leave your side,
I will never hurt your pride.
When all the chips are down,
I will always be around,
Just to be right where you are, my love.

Oh, I love you, boy.
I will never leave you out,
I will always let you in
To places no one has ever been.
Deep inside, can't you see?
I believe in you and me.
(To Bridge:)

I Believe In You And Me - 5 - 5

NOW AND FOREVER

Recorded by Richard Marx

Music and Lyrics by
RICHARD MARX
Arranged by Richard Bradley

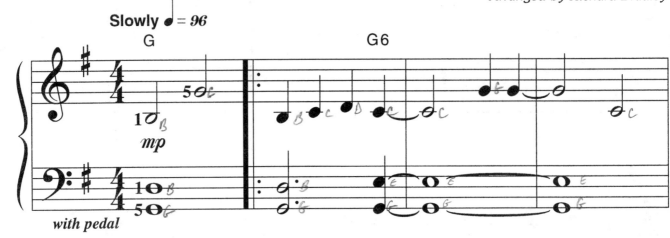

1. When - ev - er I'm wear - y _____ from the

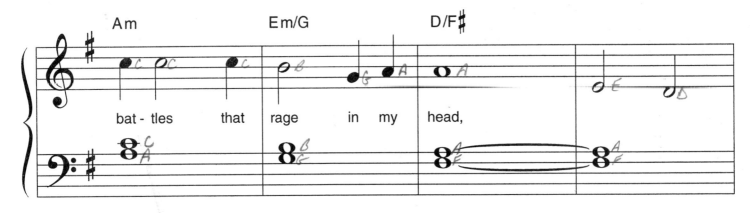

bat - tles that rage in my head,

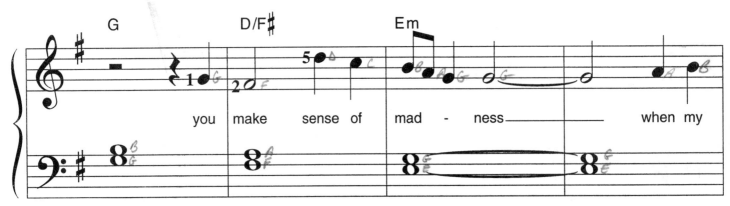

you make sense of mad - ness _____ when my

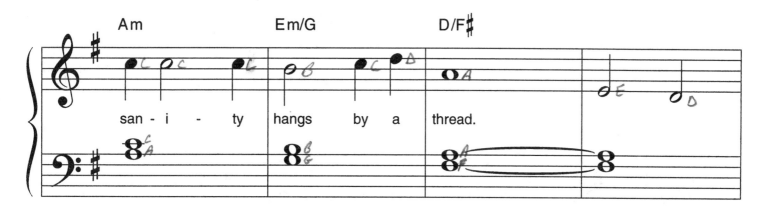

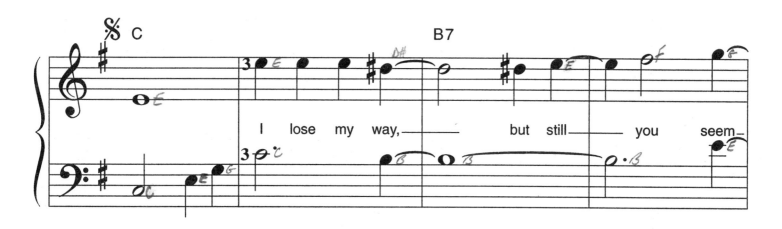

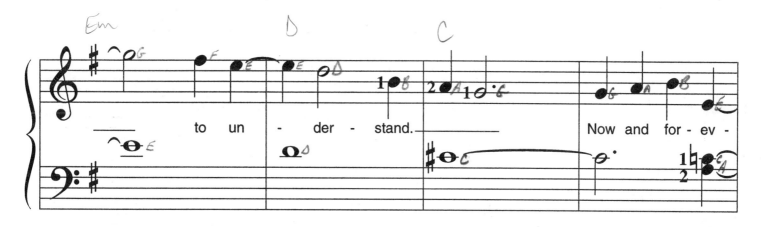

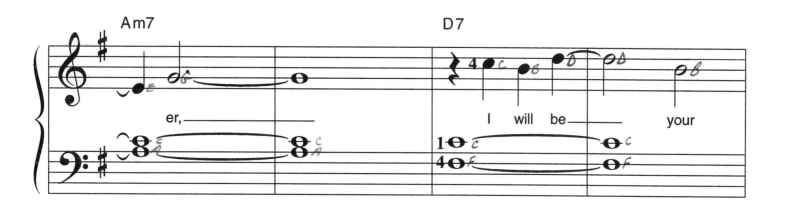

82

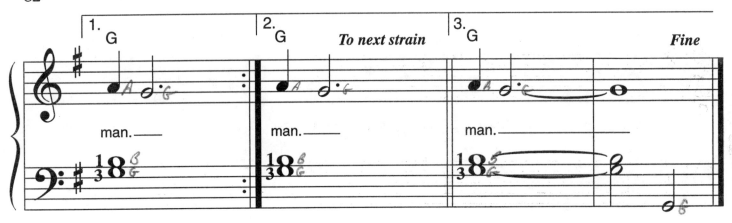

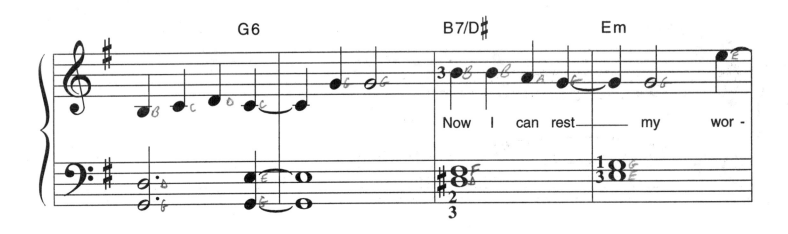

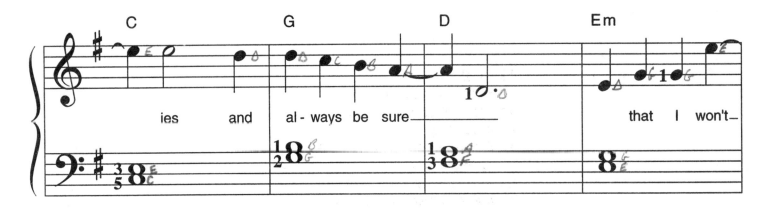

Now And Forever - 4 - 3

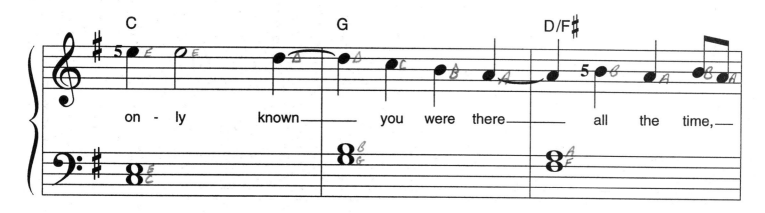

on - ly known_____ you were there_____ all the time,___

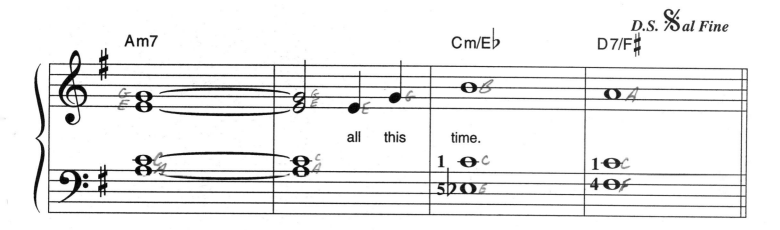

all this time.

D.S. %al Fine

Verse 2:
Sometimes I just hold you
Too caught up in me to see
I am holding a fortune
That heaven has given to me.
I'll try to show you
Each and ev'ry way I can,
Now and forever, I will be your man.

Verse 3:
Until the day the ocean
Doesn't touch the sand,
Now and forever, I will be your man.

WITHOUT YOU

Recorded by Mariah Carey

By
WILLIAM HAM and TOM EVANS
Arranged by Richard Bradley

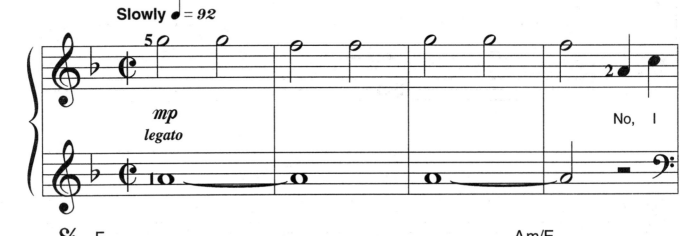

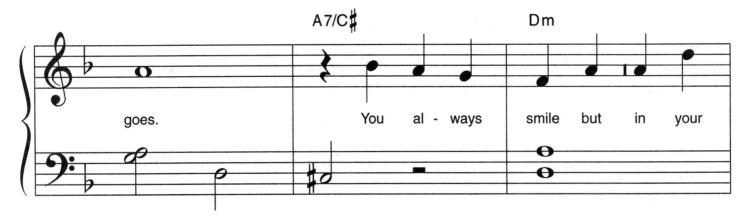

86

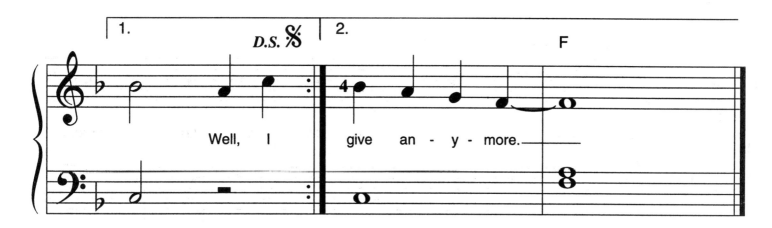

Verse 2:
No, I can't forget tomorrow
When I think of all my sorrow,
When I had you there but then I let you go.
And now it's only fair that I should let you know,
What you should know.

Verse 3:
Well, I can't forget the evening,
Or your face as you were leaving
But I guess that's just the way the story goes.
You always smile
But in your eyes your sorrow shows,
Yes it shows.

SOMEBODY'S CRYING

Recorded by Chris Isaak

Words and Music by
CHRIS ISAAK
Arranged by Richard Bradley

some - bod - y's ly - in'.   I know when

some - bod - y's ly - in'.   *To Coda* ⊕

I know that

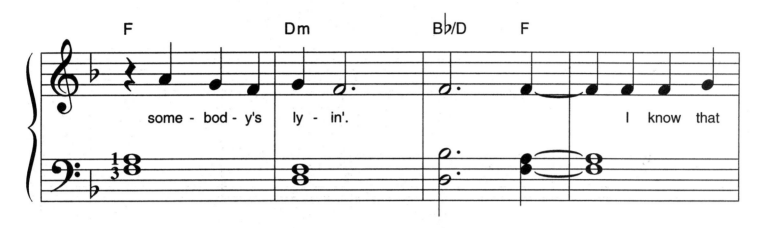

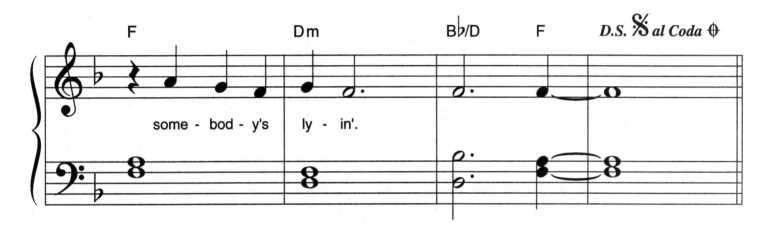

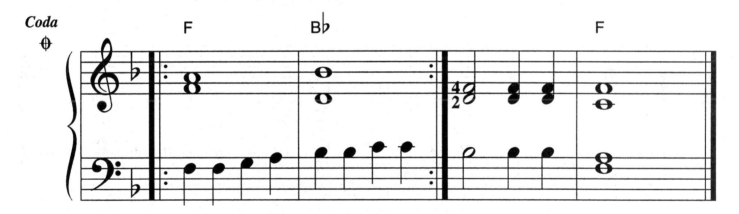

Verse 2:
I know somebody and they called your name
A million times and still you never came.
They go on loving you just the same.
I know that somebody's tryin'.

Verse 3:
Give me a sign and let me know we're through,
If you don't love me like I love you.
But if you cry at night the way I do,
I'll know that somebody's lyin'.

I BELIEVE I CAN FLY

From the Motion Picture Soundtrack "Space Jam"
Recorded by R. Kelly

Words and Music by
R. KELLY
Arranged by Richard Bradley

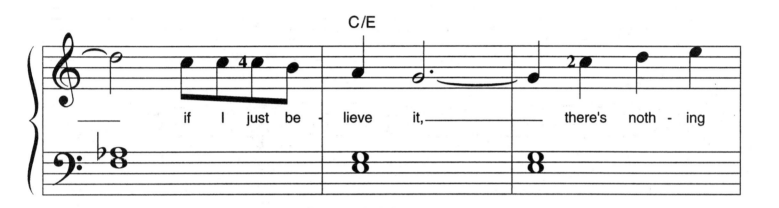

94

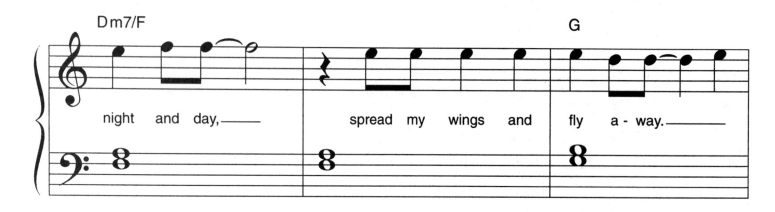

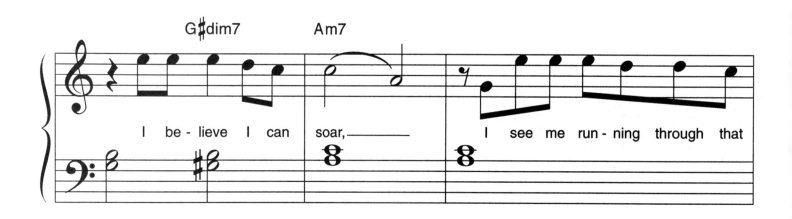

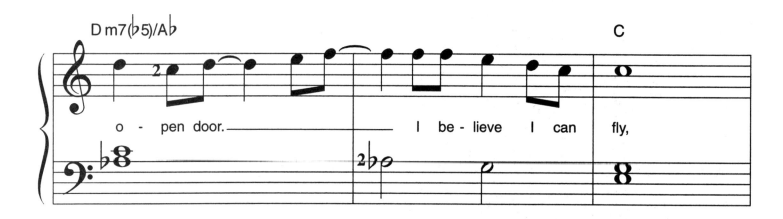

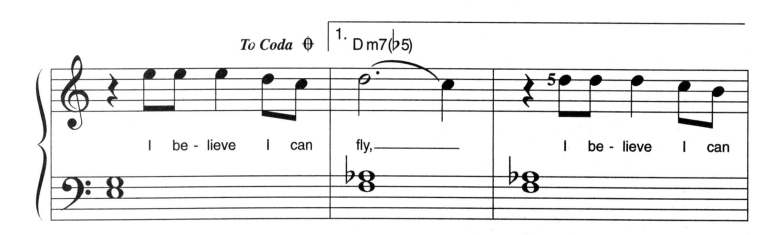

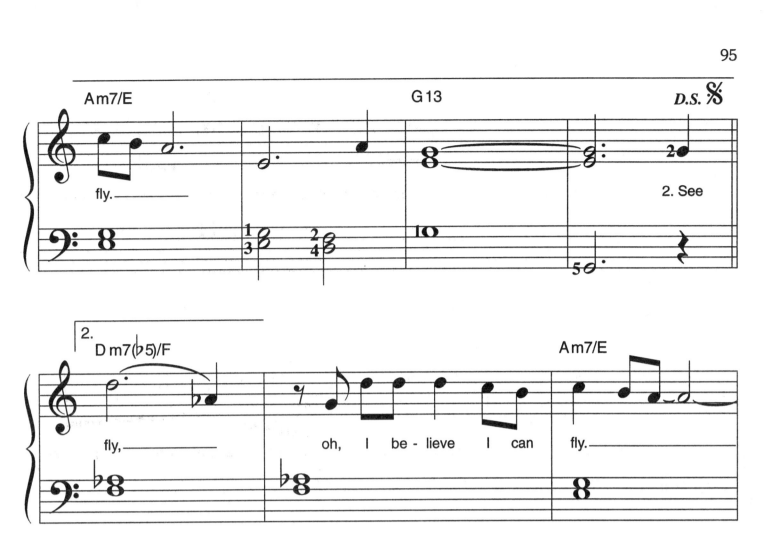

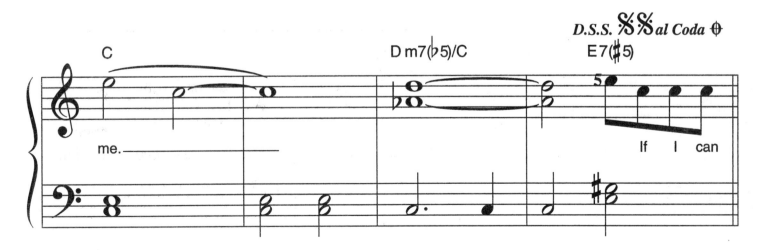

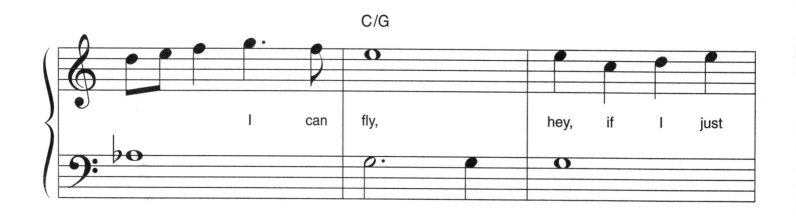

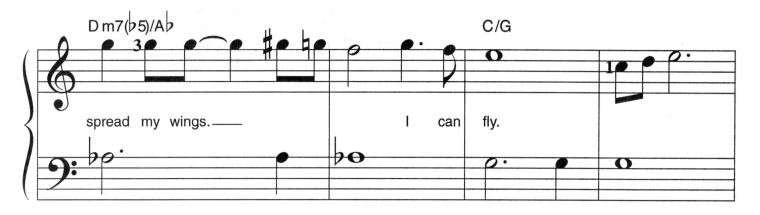

spread my wings.⸺   I can fly.

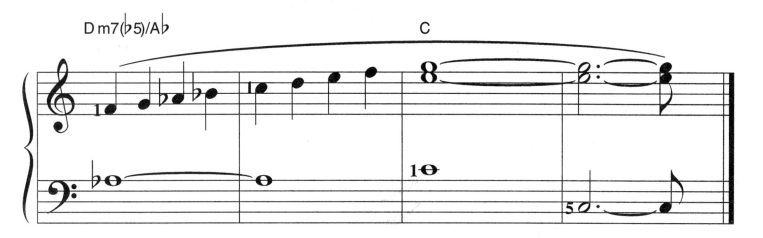

Verse 2:
See, I was on the verge of breaking down.
Sometimes silence can seem so loud.
There are miracles in life I must achieve,
But first I know it starts inside of me.

YOU GOT IT

From the Motion Picture "Boys On The Side"
Recorded by Bonnie Raitt

Words and Music by
ROY ORBISON, JEFF LYNNE
and TOM PETTY
Arranged by Richard Bradley

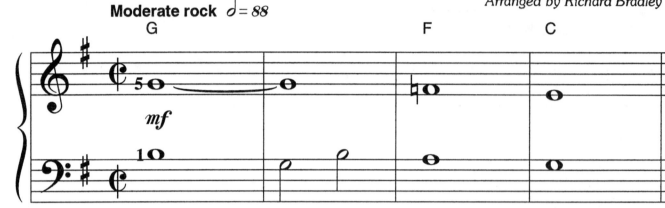

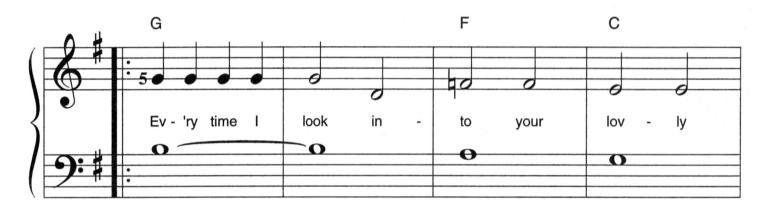

Ev - 'ry time I look in - to your lov - ly

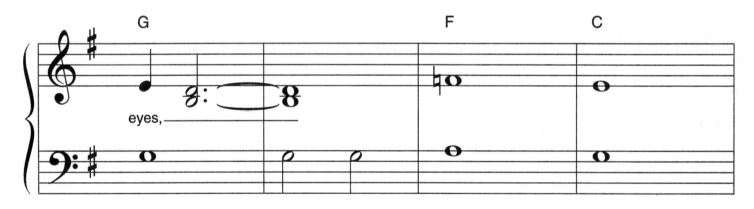

eyes,

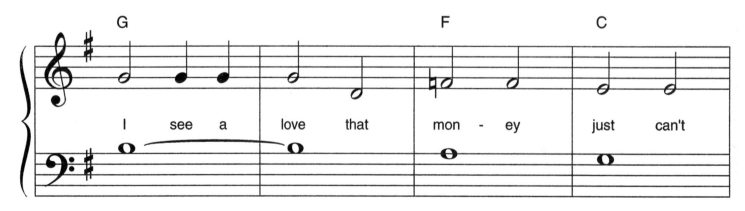

I see a love that mon - ey just can't

You Got It - 5 - 1

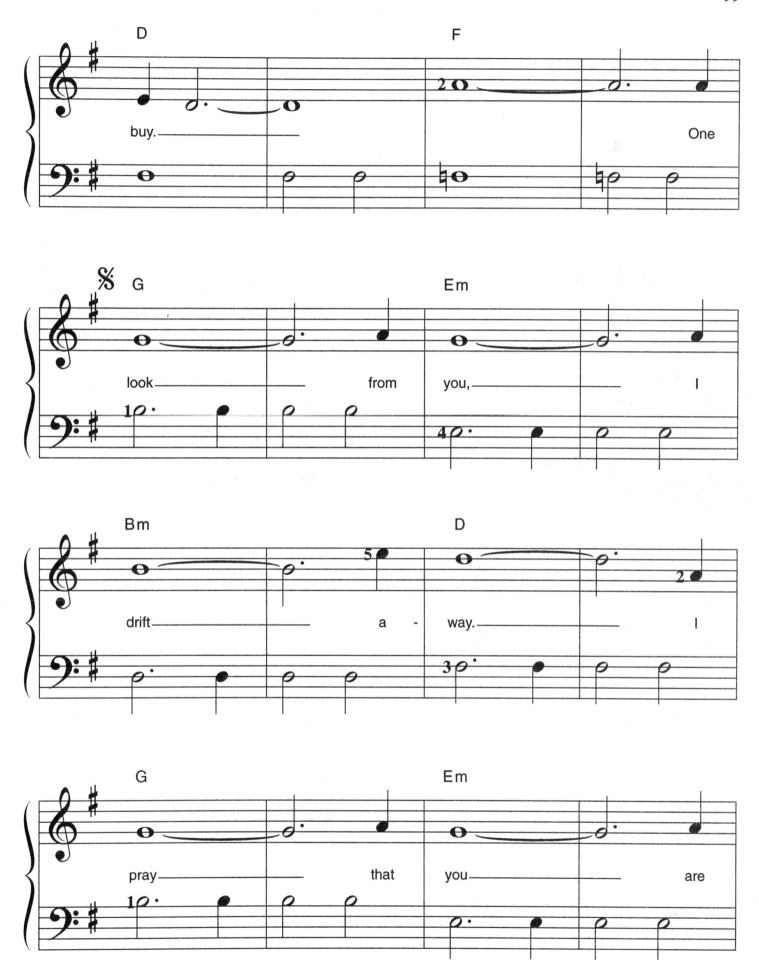

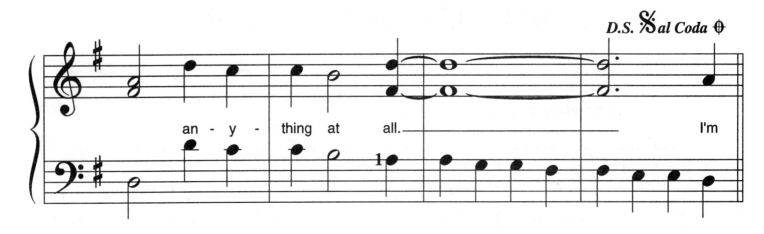

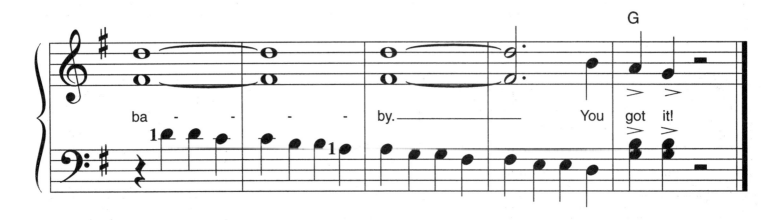

Verse 2:
Ev'ry time I hold you, I begin to understand.
Ev'ry thing about you tells me you're my man.
I live my life to be with you.
No one can do the things you do.

Verse 3:
I'm glad to give my love to you.
I know you feel the way I do.

I WILL ALWAYS LOVE YOU

Recorded by Whitney Houston

Words and Music by
DOLLY PARTON
Arranged by Richard Bradley

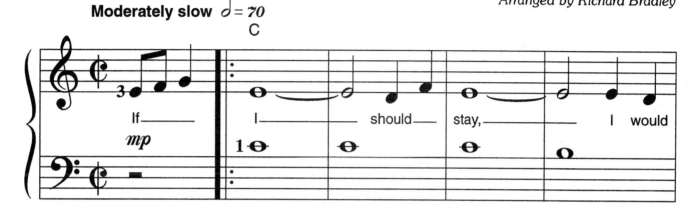

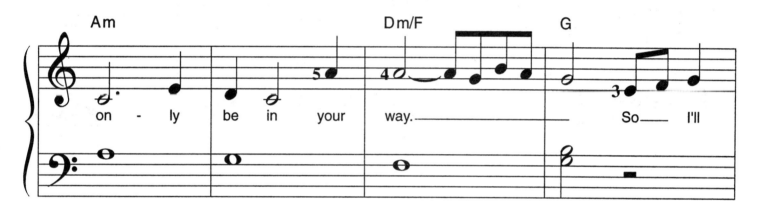

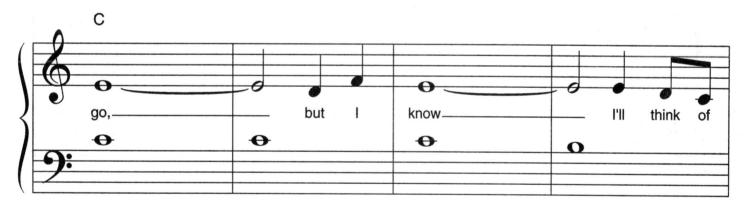

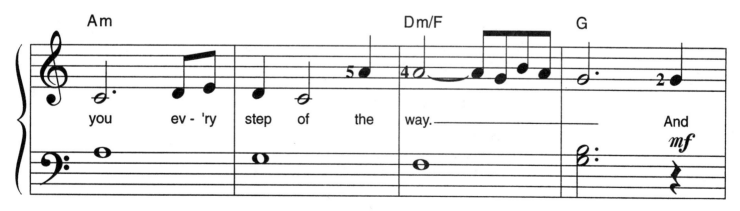

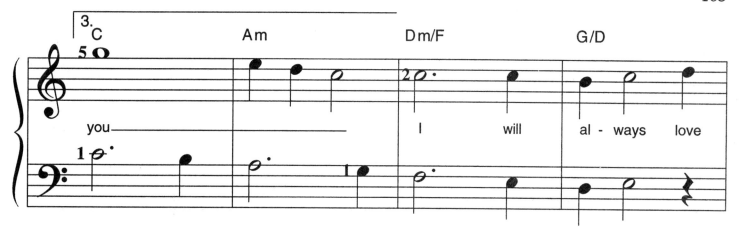

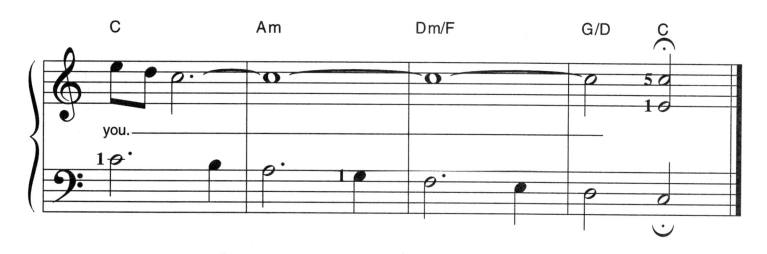

Verse 2:
Bittersweet memories that is all
I'm taking with me.
So, goodbye. Please, don't cry.
We both know I'm not what you, you need.
And I will always love you.
I will always love you.

Verse 3:
I hope life treats you kind
And I hope you have all you've dreamed of.
And I wish to you, joy and happiness.
But above all this,
I wish you love.

I Will Always Love You - 3 - 3

YOU'LL SEE

Recorded by Madonna

Words and Music by
MADONNA CICCONE
and DAVID FOSTER
Arranged by Richard Bradley

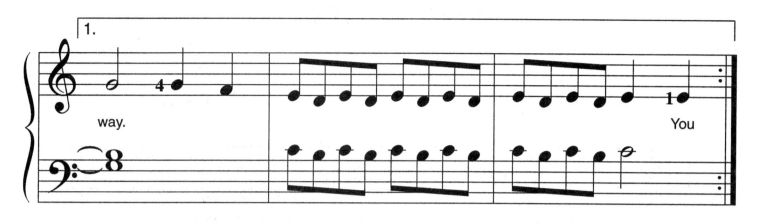

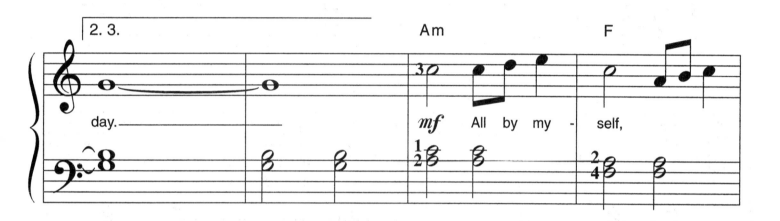

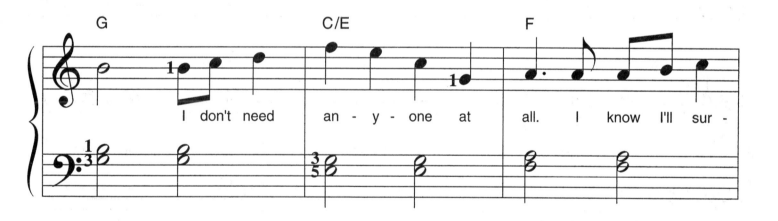

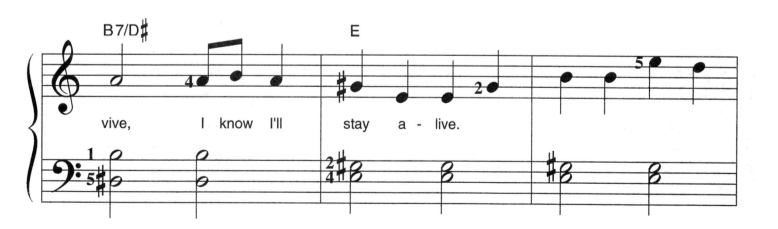

Coda

mp You'll see.

You'll see, p you'll see.

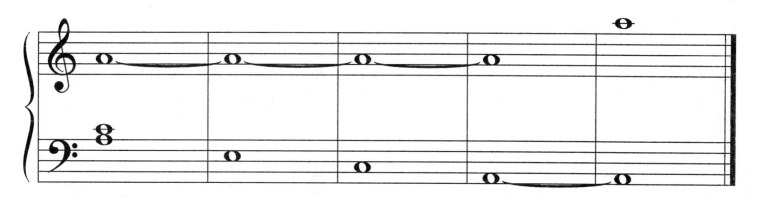

Verse 2:
You think that I can never laugh again, you'll see.
You think that you've destroyed my faith in love.
You think after all you've done,
I'll never find my way back home.
You'll see, somehow, someday.

Verse 3:
You think that you are strong but you are weak, you'll see.
It takes more strength to cry, admit defeat.
I have truth on my side, you only have deceit.
You'll see, somehow, someday.

Chorus 3:
All by myself, I don't need anyone at all.
I know I'll survive, I know I'll stay alive.
I'll stand on my own, I won't need anyone this time.
It will be mine, no one can take it from me, you'll see.

You'll See - 4 - 4

BLESSED

Recorded by Elton John

Words and Music by
ELTON JOHN and BERNIE TAUPIN
Arranged by Richard Bradley

Blessed - 6 - 1

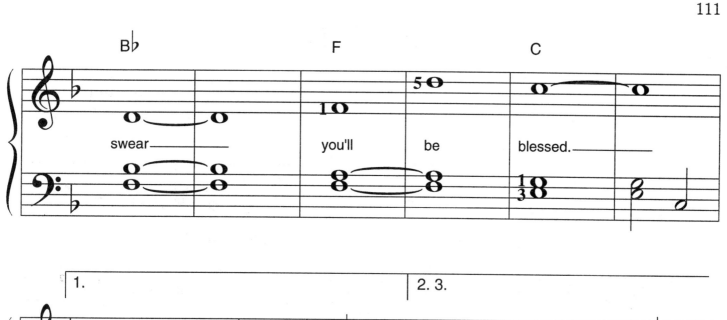

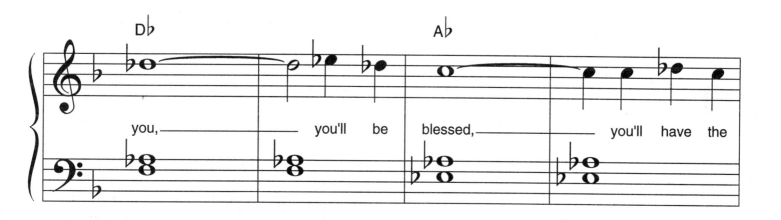

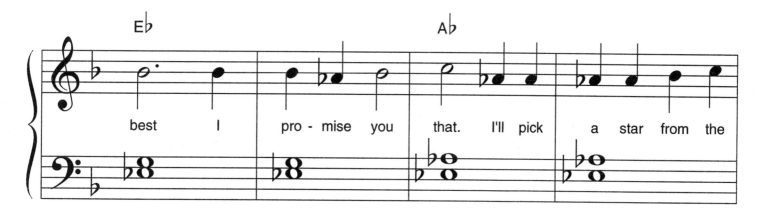

112

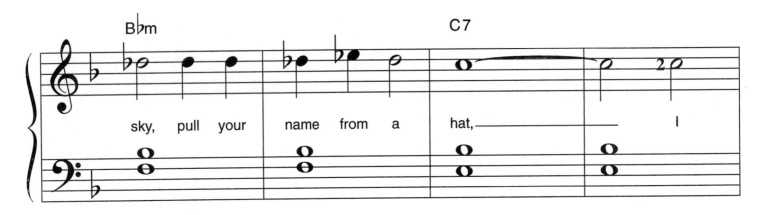

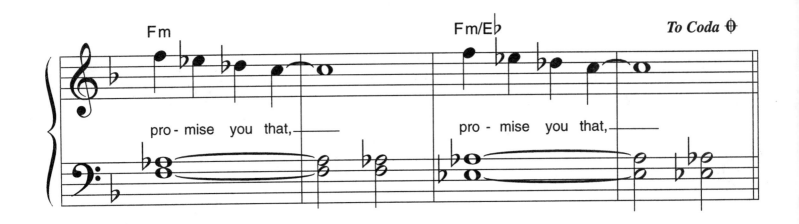

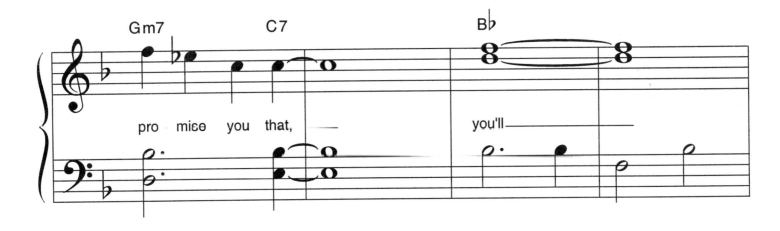

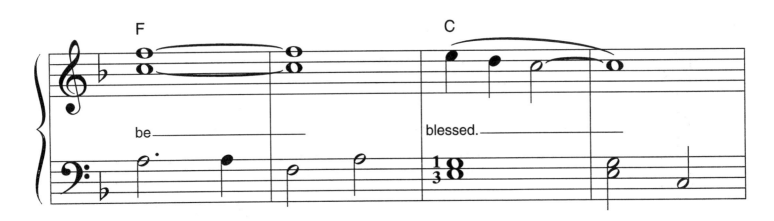

Blessed - 6 - 3

You,———— you'll be blessed,———— you'll have the

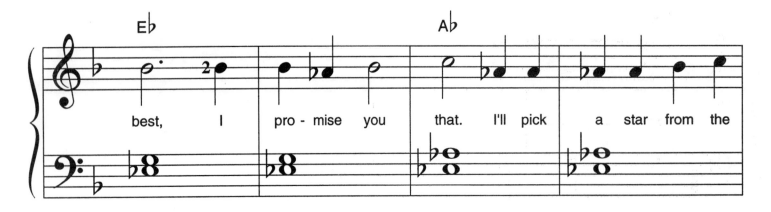

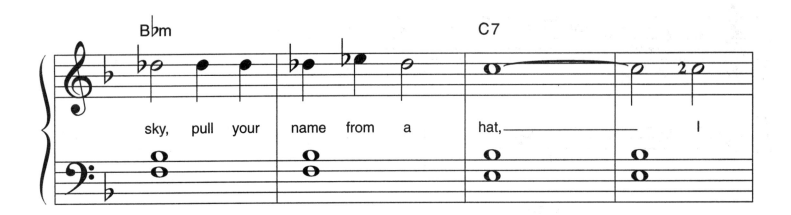

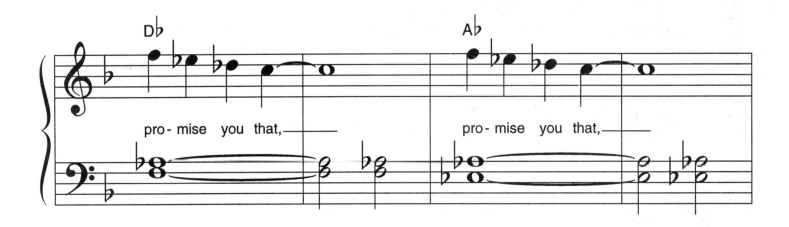

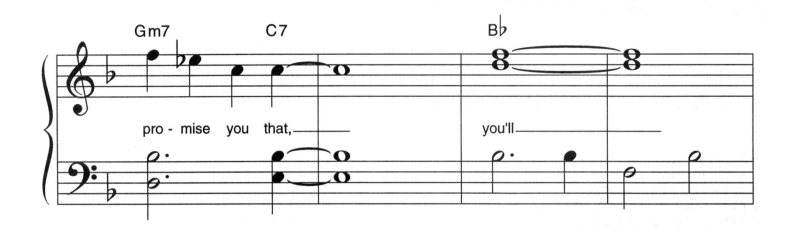

Verse 2:
I know you're still just a dream,
Your eyes might be green,
Or the bluest that I've ever seen,
Anyway you'll be blessed.

Verse 3:
I need you, before I'm too old,
To have and to hold,
To walk with you and watch you grow,
And know that you're blessed.

Blessed - 6 - 6

TEARS IN HEAVEN

Recorded by Eric Clapton

Words and Music by
WILL JENNINGS and ERIC CLAPTON
Arranged by Richard Bradley

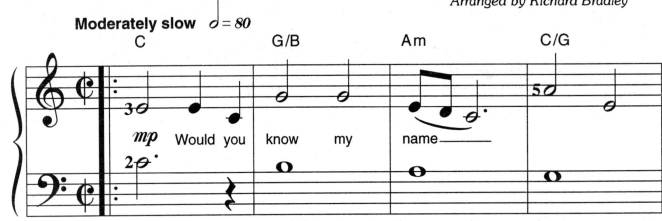

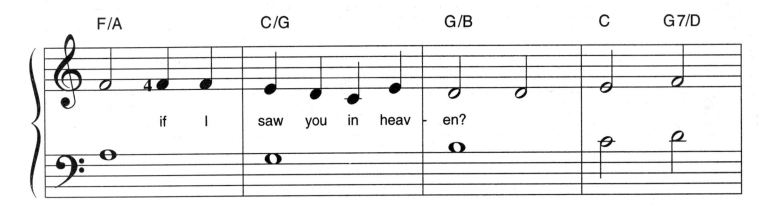

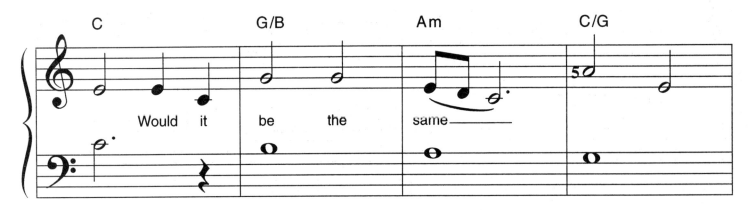

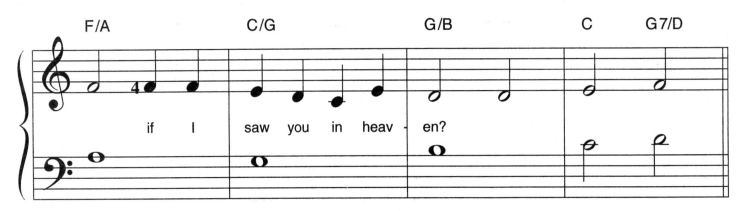

Tears In Heaven - 4 - 1

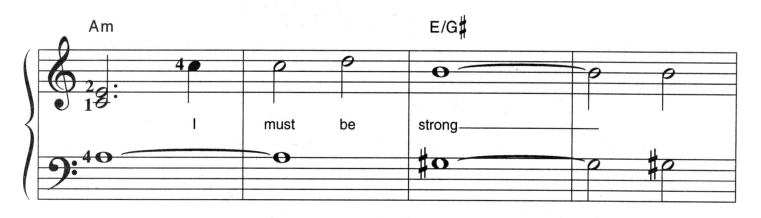

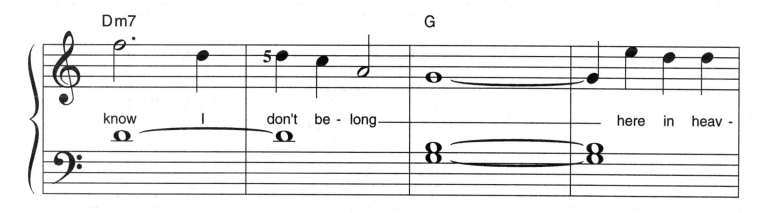

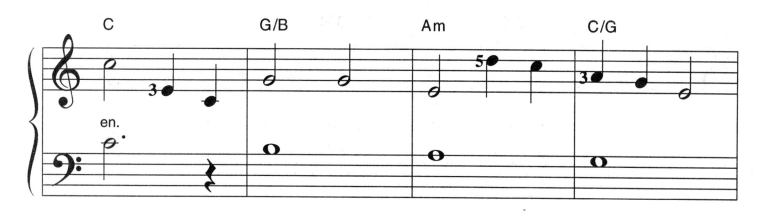

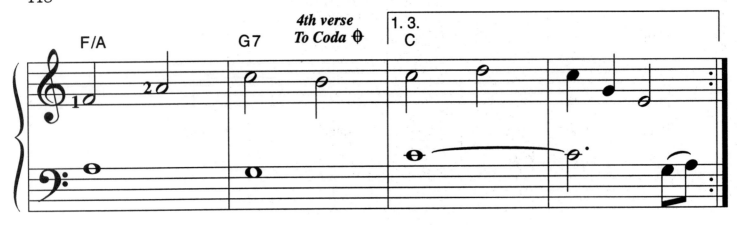

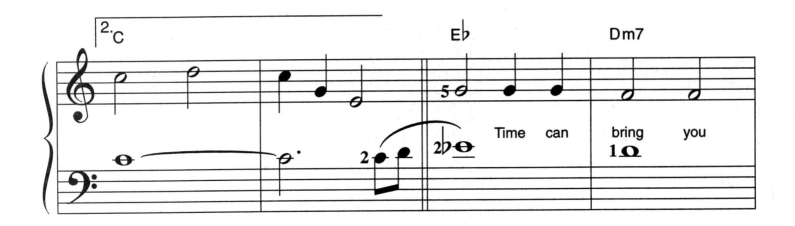

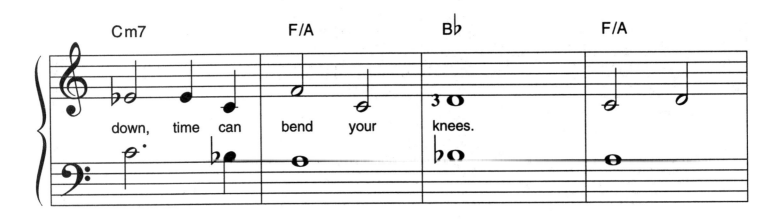

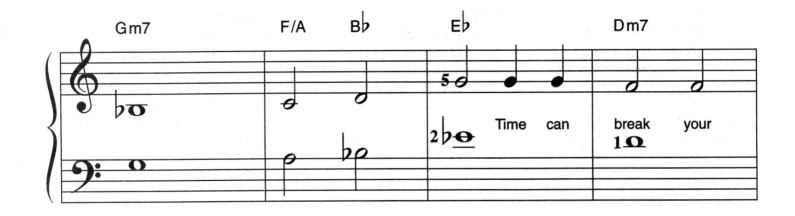

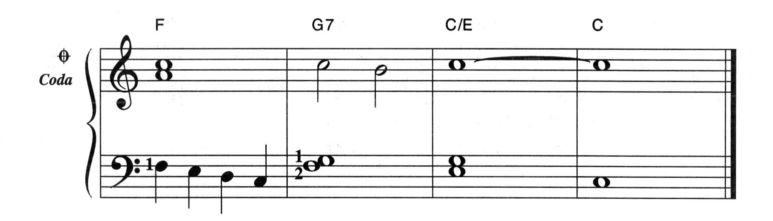

Verse: 2
Would you hold my hand
If I saw you in heaven?
Would you help me stand
If I saw you in heaven?
I'll find my way
Through night and day,
'Cause I know I just can't stay
Here in heaven.

Verse 3:
Instrumental solo . . .
Beyond the door
There's peace I'm sure.
And I know there'll be no more
Tears in heaven.

Verse 4:
Would you know my name
If I saw you in heaven?
Would you be the same
If I saw you in heaven?
I must be strong and carry on,
'Cause I know I don't belong
Here in heaven.

REACH

Recorded by Gloria Estefan

Words and Music by
GLORIA ESTEFAN
and DIANE WARREN
Arranged by Richard Bradley

Some dreams live on in time for-ever.

Those dreams, you want with all your heart. And I'll

Reach - 4 - 1

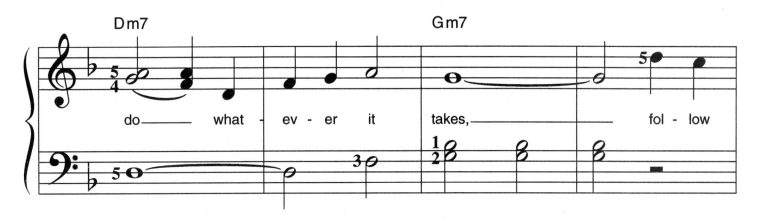

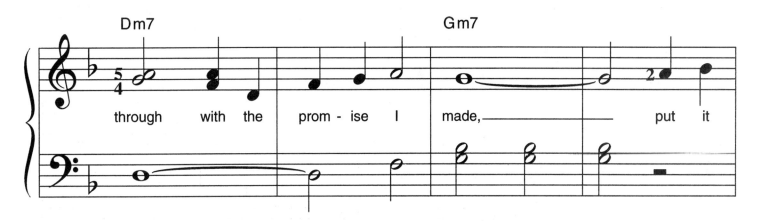

Reach - 4 - 2

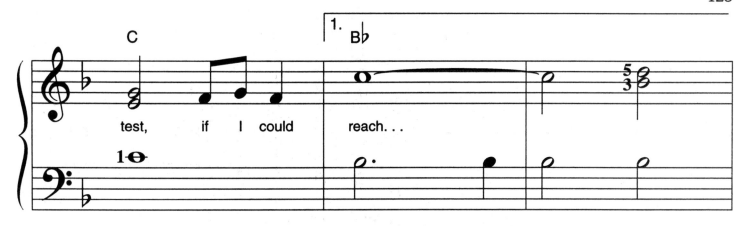

test, if I could reach...

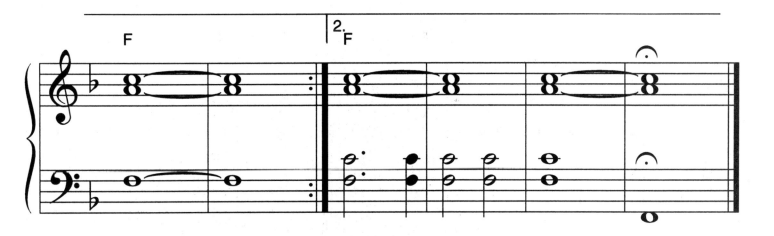

Verse 2:
Some days are meant to be remembered.
Those days we rise above the stars.
So, I'll go the distance this time,
Seeing more the higher I climb
That the more I believe,
All the more that this dream will be mine.

THE WIND BENEATH MY WINGS

Recorded by Bette Midler

Words and Music by
LARRY HENLEY and JEFF SILBAR
Arranged by Richard Bradley

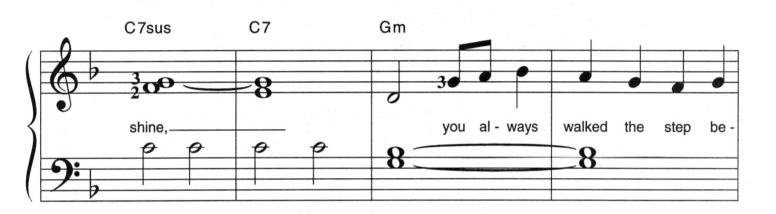

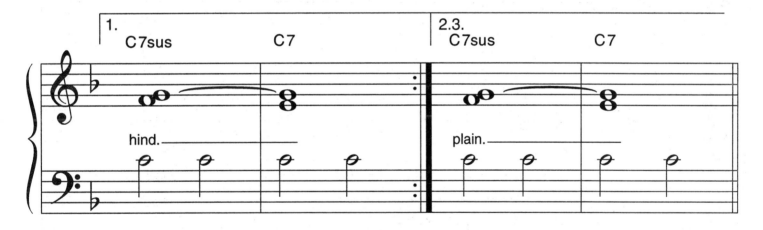

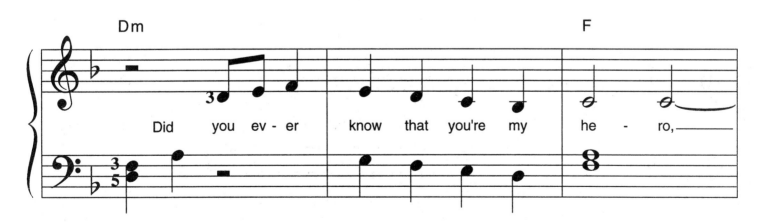

The Wind Beneath My Wings - 4 - 2

126

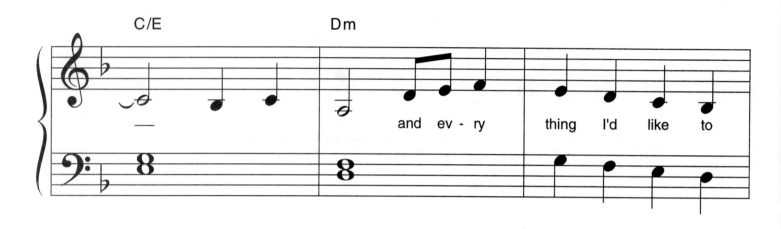

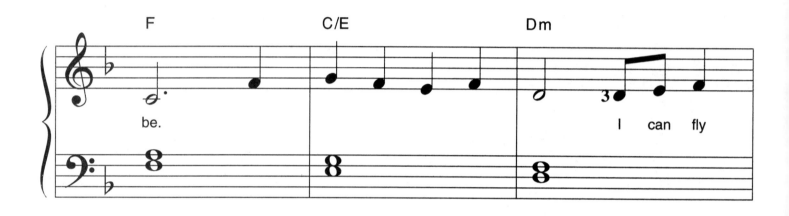

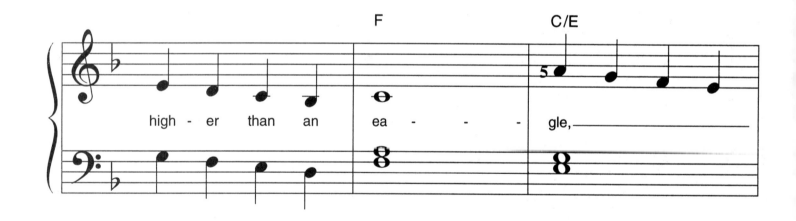

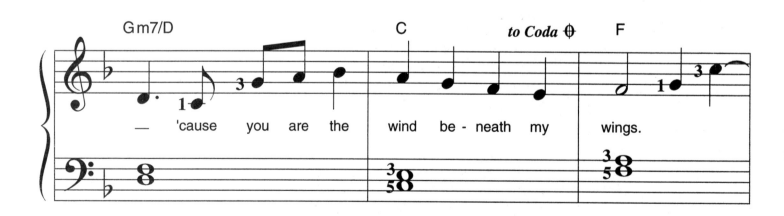

The Wind Beneath My Wings - 4 - 3

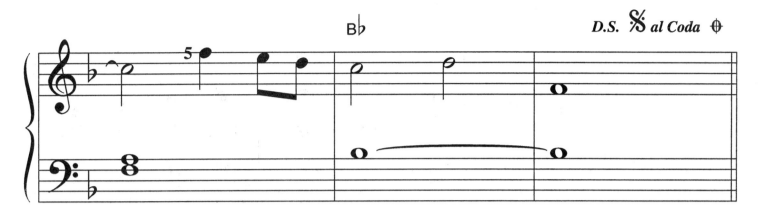

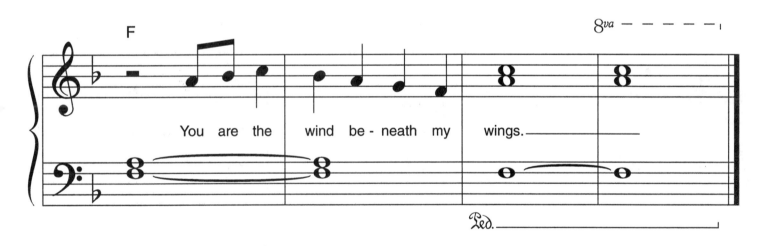

Verse 2
I was the one with all the glory,
While you were the one with all the strength,
Only a face without a name,
I never once heard you complain.

Verse 3:
It might have appeared to go unnoticed
That I've got it all here in my heart.
I want you to know I know the truth,
I would be nothin' without you.

The Wind Beneath My Wings - 4 - 4

I DON'T WANT TO

Recorded by Toni Braxton

Words and Music by
R. KELLY
Arranged by Richard Bradley

real-ly don't feel like talk-ing on the phone,

and I real-ly don't feel like com-pa-ny at

home._____ Late-ly, I don't want to do the

things I used to do, ba-by, since

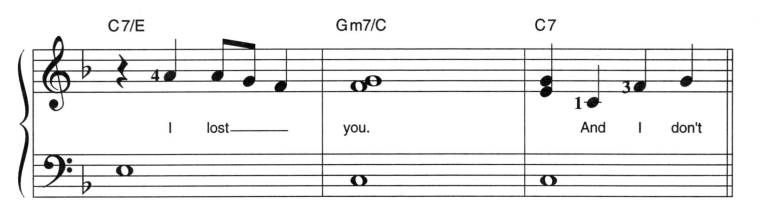

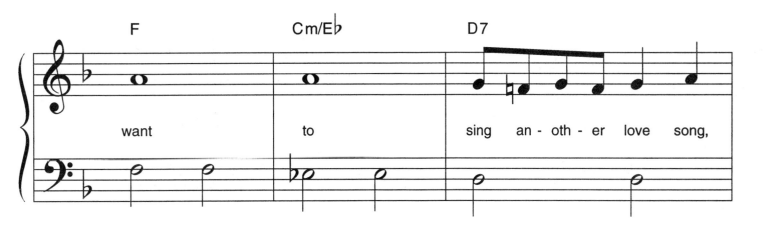

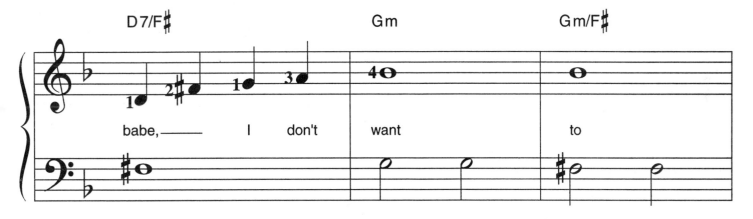

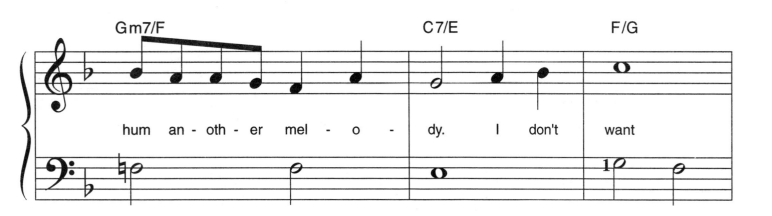

130

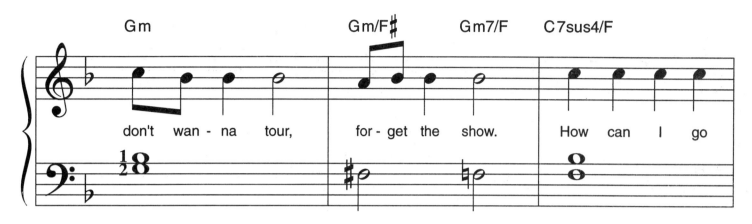

don't wan - na tour, for - get the show. How can I go

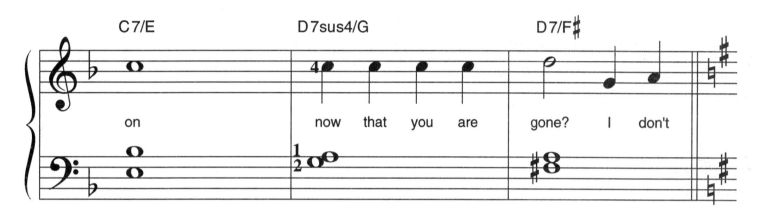

on now that you are gone? I don't

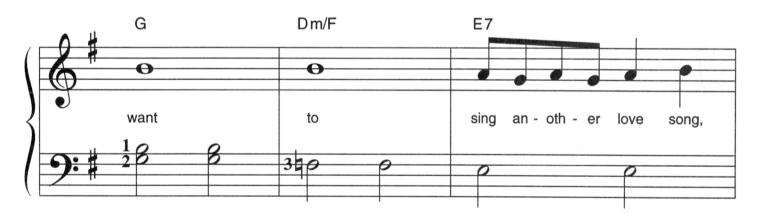

want to sing an - oth - er love song,

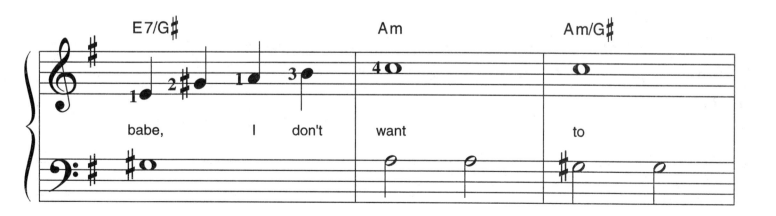

babe, I don't want to

I Don't Want To - 5 - 4

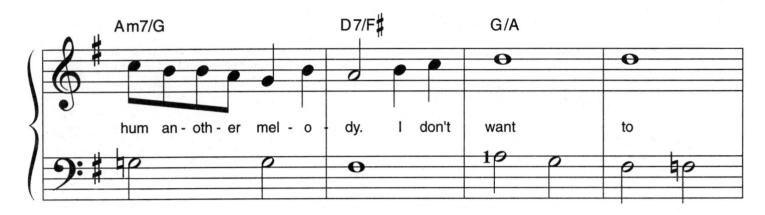

hum an - oth - er mel - o - dy. I don't want to

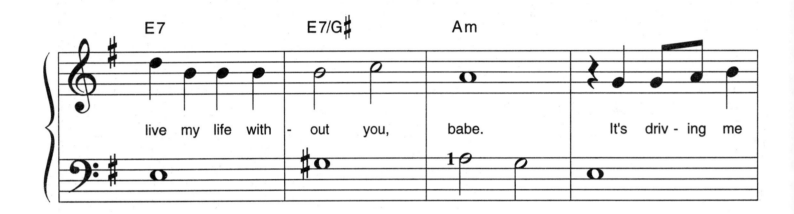

live my life with - out you, babe. It's driv - ing me

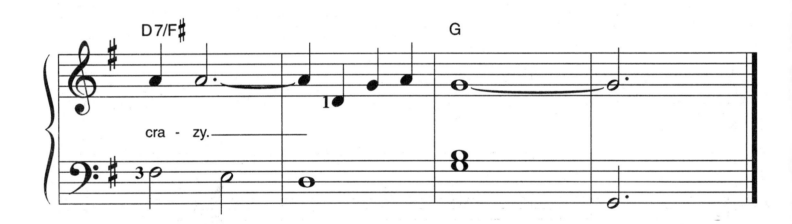

cra - zy.

Verse 2:
I really don't feel like smiling anymore,
And I haven't had the peace to sleep at all.
Ever since you went away, babe,
My whole life has changed.
I don't wanna love and I don't wanna live.

RUN TO YOU

Recorded by Whitney Houston

Words and Music by
JUD FRIEDMAN and ALLAN RICH
Arranged by Richard Bradley

Run To You - 5 - 1

134

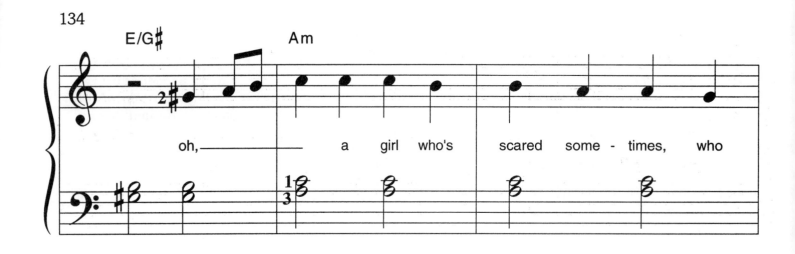

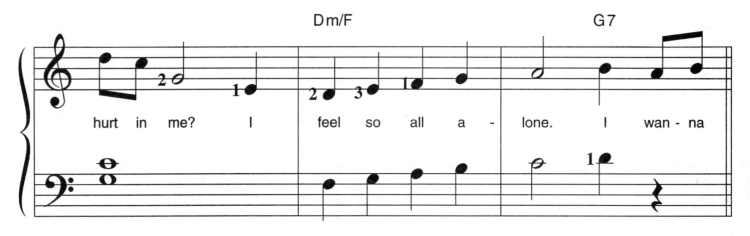

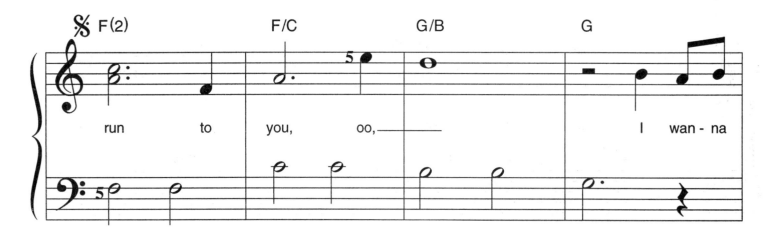

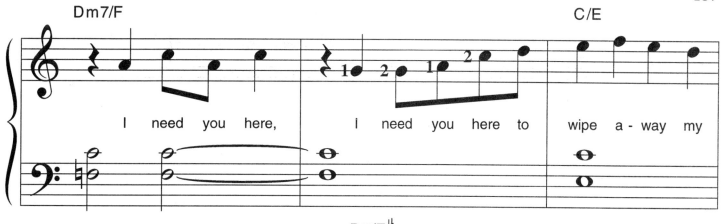

I need you here, I need you here to wipe a - way my

tears_____ to kiss a - way my fears._____ If you

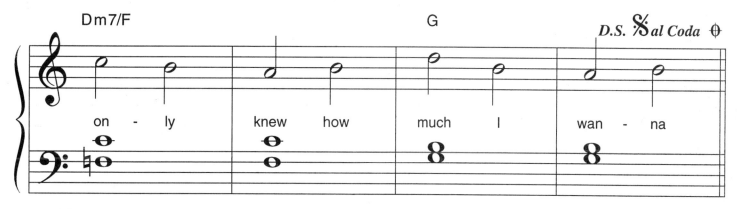

on - ly knew how much I wan - na

D.S. %al Coda

Coda

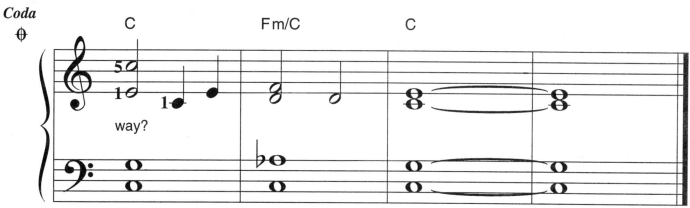

way?

Verse 2:
Each day, each day I play the role
Of someone always in control.
But at night, I come home and turn the key,
There's nobody there, no on cares for me.
Oh, what's the sense of trying hard to find your dreams?
Without someone to share them with,
Tell me what does it mean?

PLEASE FORGIVE ME

Recorded by Bryan Adams

Words and Music by
BRYAN ADAMS and
ROBERT JOHN "MUTT" LANGE
Arranged by Richard Bradley

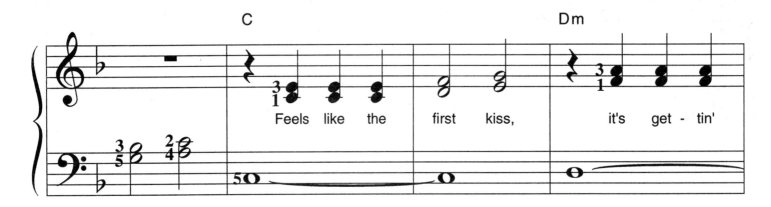

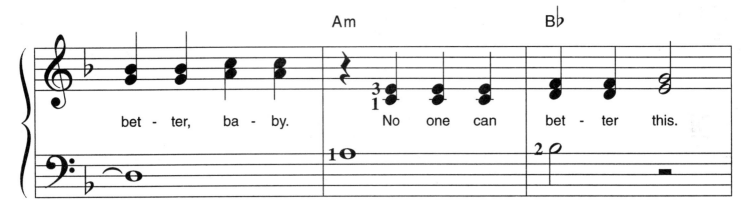

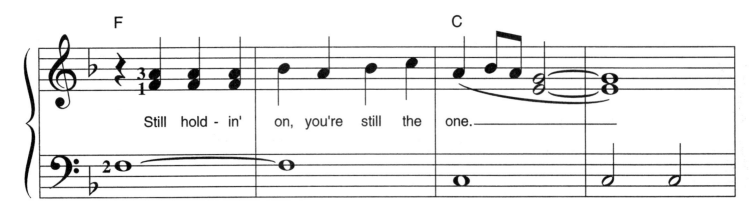

Please Forgive Me - 4 - 1

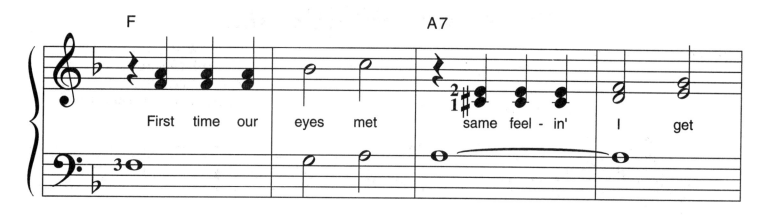

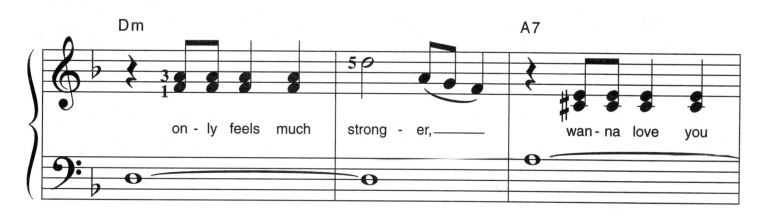

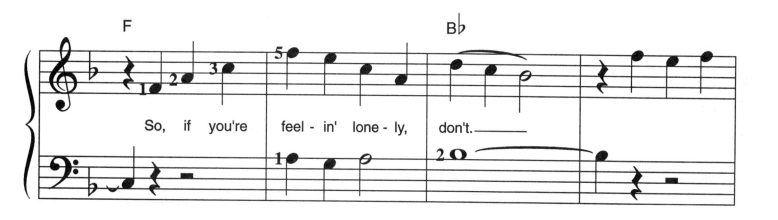

140

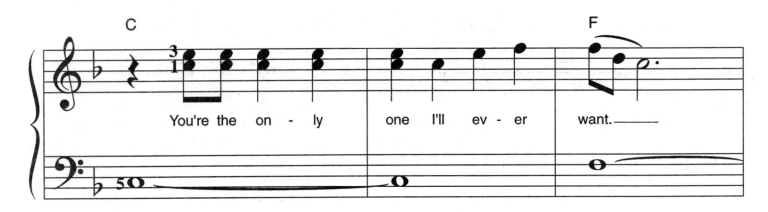

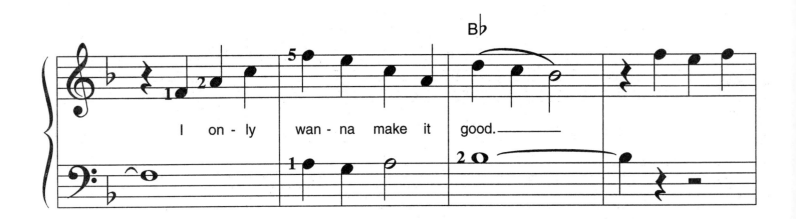

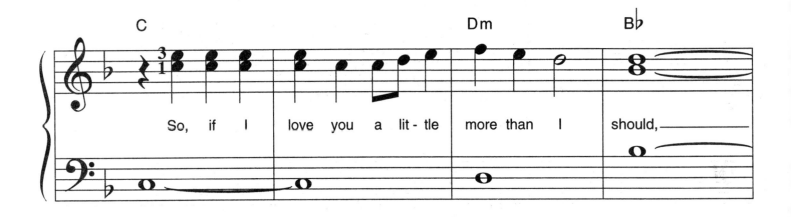

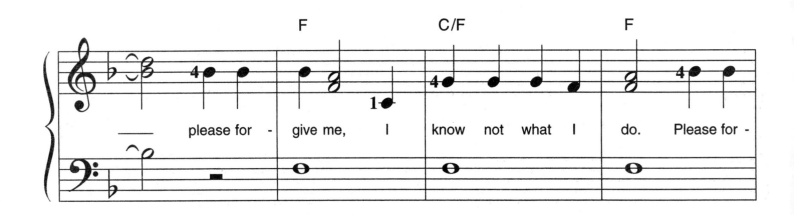

Please Forgive Me - 4 - 3

141

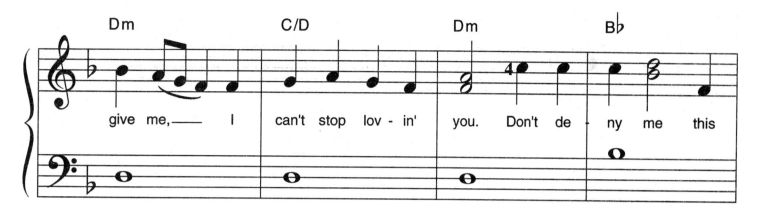

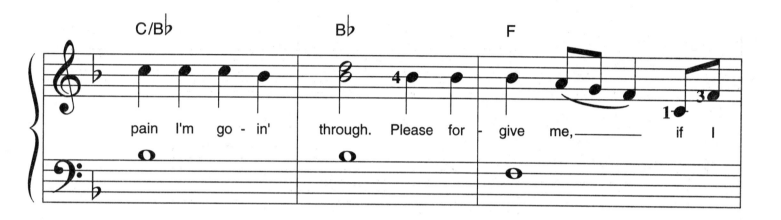

KILLING ME SOFTLY
(WITH HIS SONG)

Recorded by Fugees

Words by NORMAN GIMBEL
Music by CHARLES FOX
Arranged by Richard Bradley

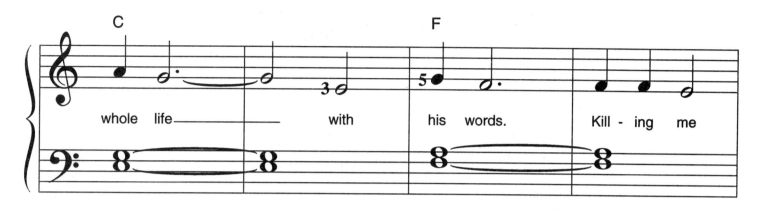

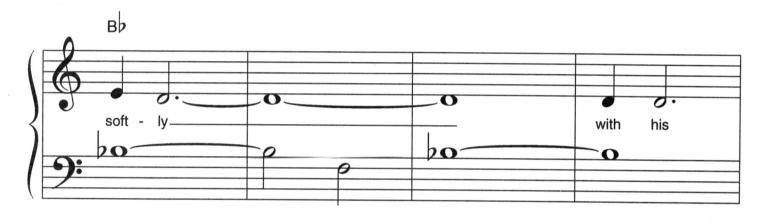

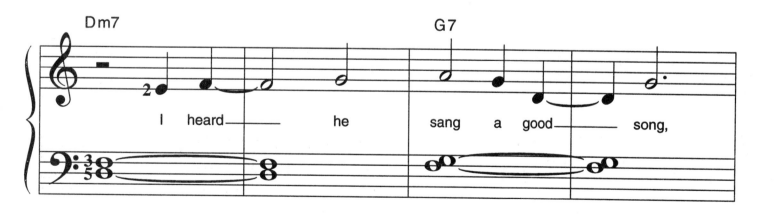

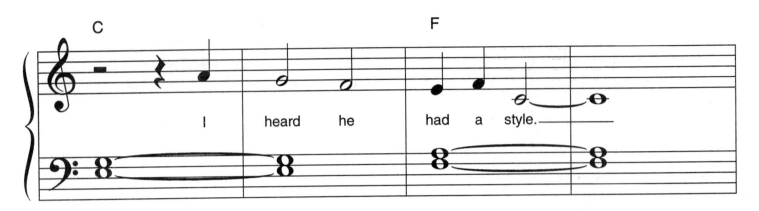

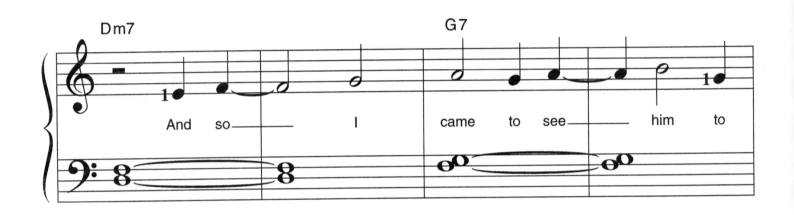

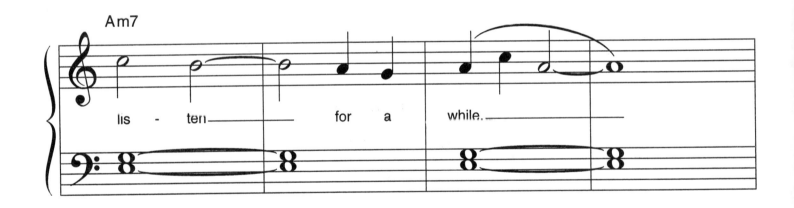

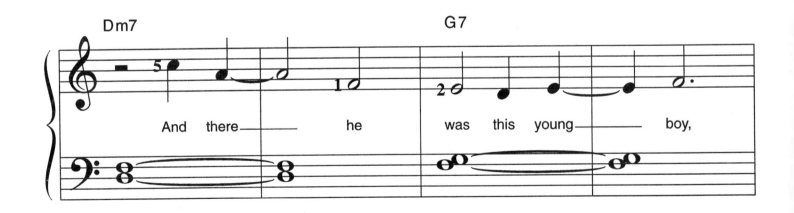

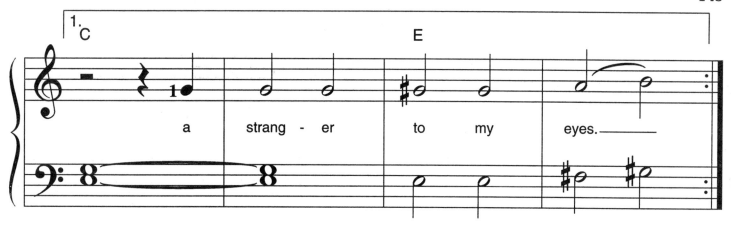

a strang - er to my eyes.

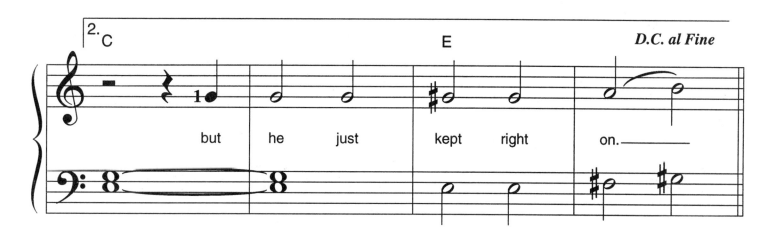

but he just kept right on.

D.C. al Fine

Verse 2:
I felt all flush with fever,
Embarassed by the crowd.
I felt he found my letters
And read each one out loud.
I prayed that he would finish,
But he just kept right on.

WORDS GET IN THE WAY

Recorded by Gloria Estefan

Words and Music by
GLORIA ESTEFAN
Arranged by Richard Bradley

Moderately slow ♩ = 76

re - a - lize you're see - ing some - one new. I don't be - lieve she knows you like I do; your tem - per - ment - al mood - y side, the one you al - ways try to hide from me.

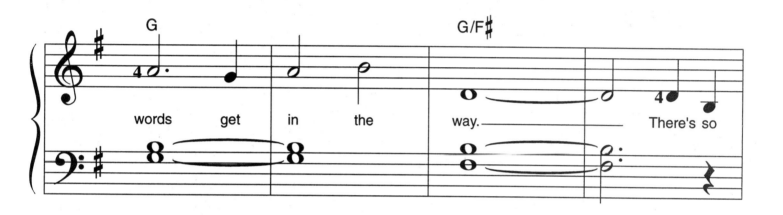

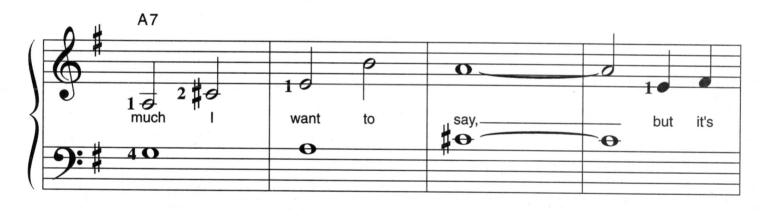

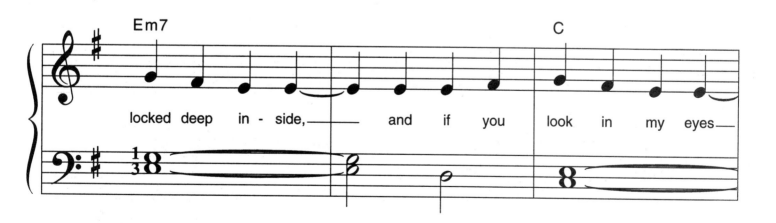

Words Get In The Way - 4 - 2

148

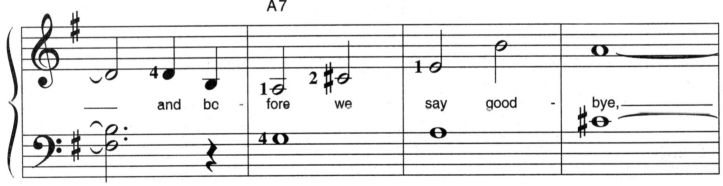

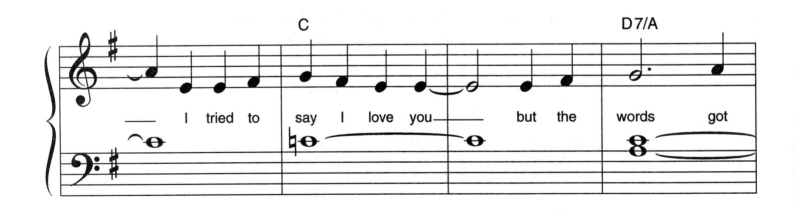

Words Get In The Way - 4 - 3

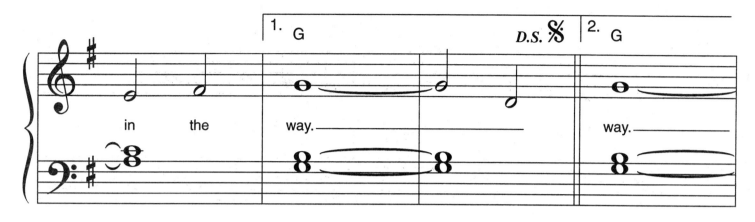

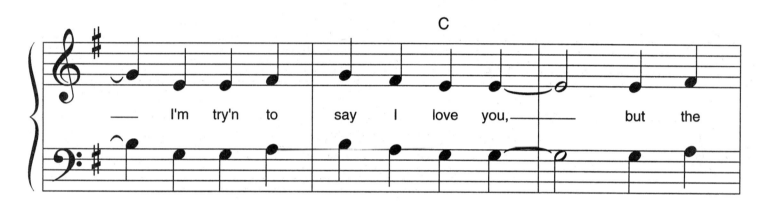

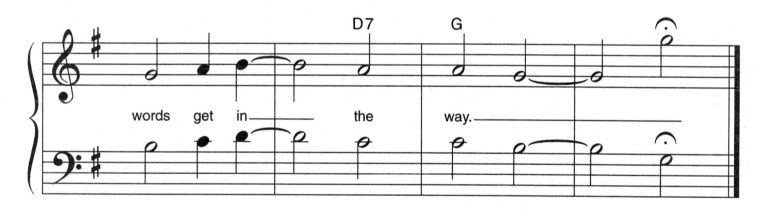

Verse 2:
But I know when you have something on your mind.
You've been trying to tell me for the longest time.
And before you break my heart in two,
There's something I've been trying to say to you.
(To Chorus:)

Verse 3:
Your heart has always been an open door,
But baby, I don't even know you any more.
And despite the fact it's hurting me,
I know the time has come to set you free.
(To Chorus:)

Words Get In The Way - 4 - 4

THE SWEETEST DAYS

Recorded by Vanessa Williams

Words and Music by
WENDY WALDMAN, JON LIND
and PHIL GALDSTON
Arranged by Richard Bradley

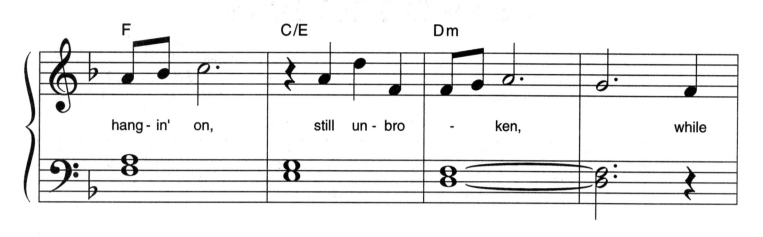

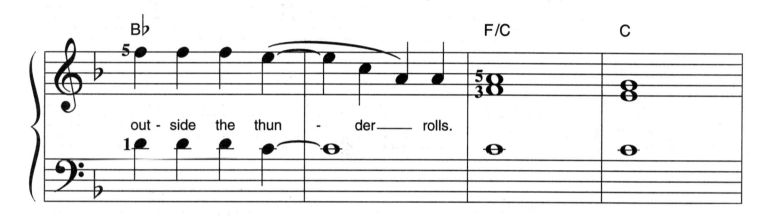

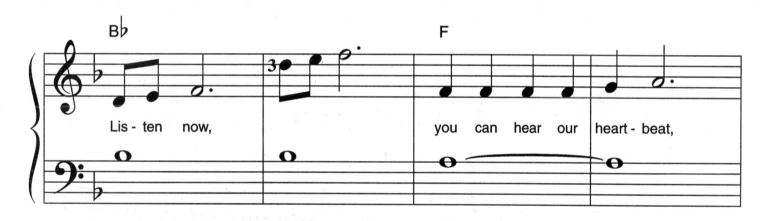

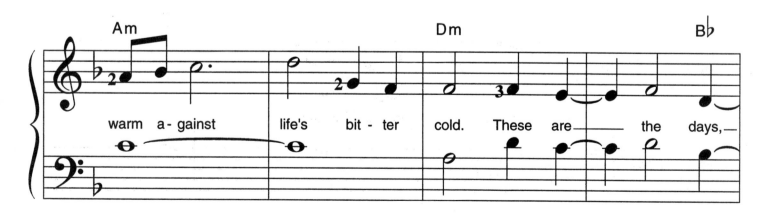

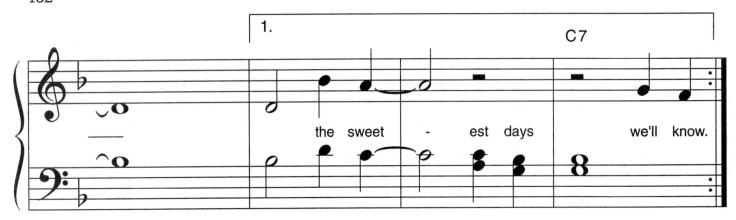

the sweet - est days we'll know.

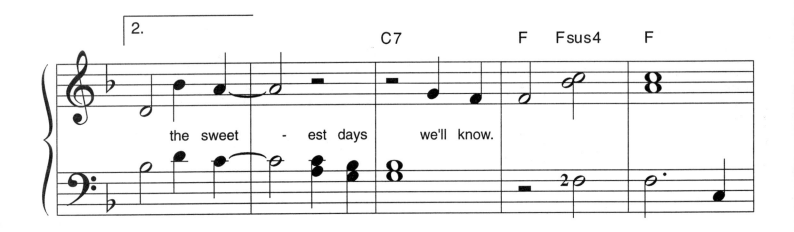

the sweet - est days we'll know.

So we'll whis - per our dreams

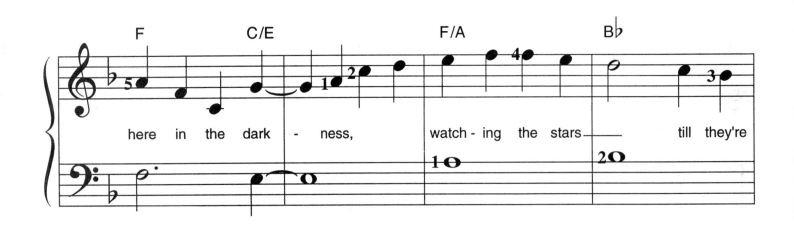

here in the dark - ness, watch - ing the stars till they're

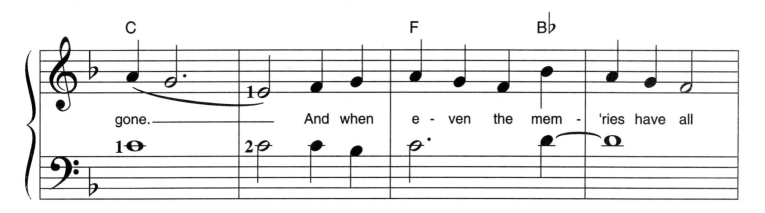

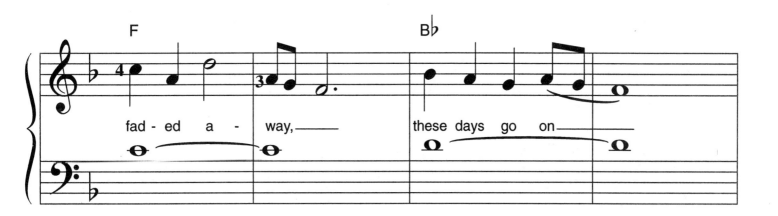

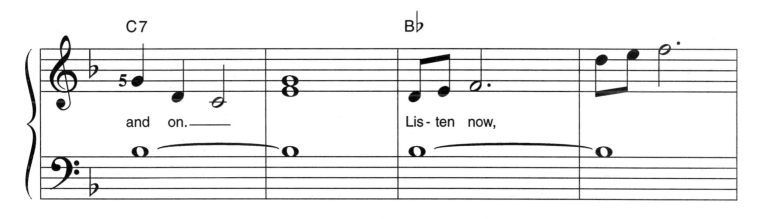

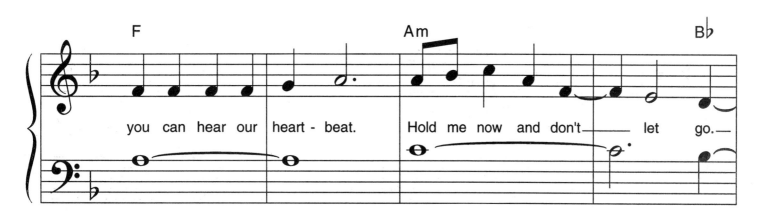

(These are _____ the days.) _____ Ev - 'ry day is the sweet -

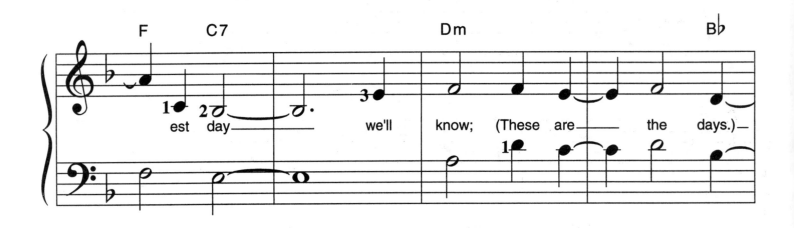

est day _____ we'll know; (These are _____ the days.) _____

the sweet - est days _____ we'll _____

Verse 2:
There are times that scare me.
You rattle the house like the wind.
Both of us so unbending,
We battle the fear we feel.
All the while life is rushing by us.
Hold it now and don't let go.
These are the days,
The sweetest days we'll know.

HERO

Recorded by Mariah Carey

Words and Music by
MARIAH CAREY and
WALTER AFANASIEFF
Arranged by Richard Bradley

Moderately slow ♩ = 74

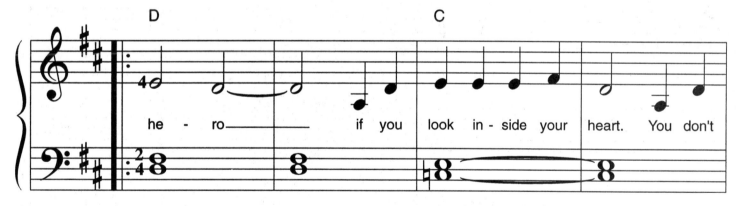

156

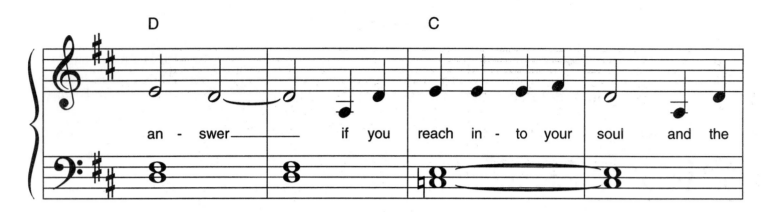

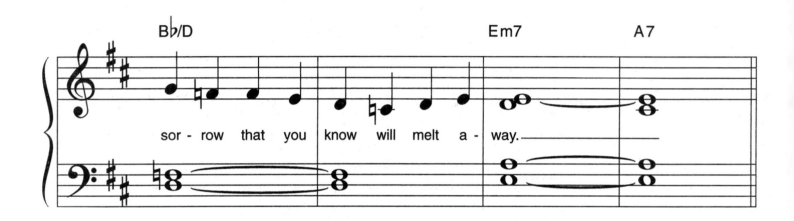

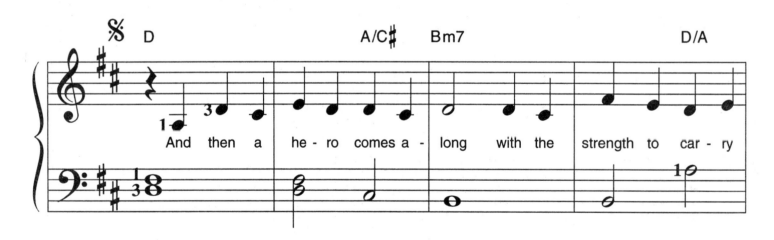

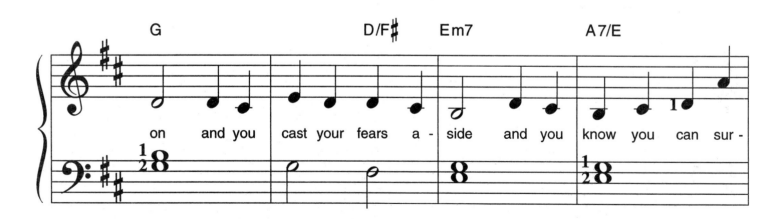

Hero - 5 - 2

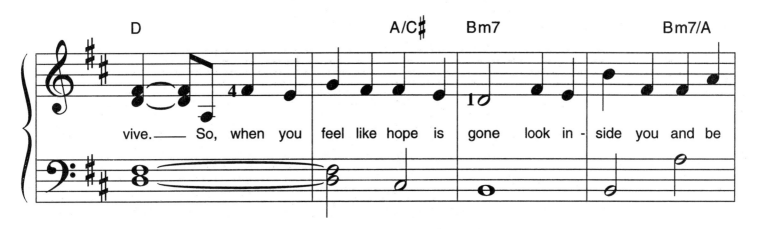

D   A/C♯   Bm7   Bm7/A

vive.— So, when you feel like hope is gone look in - side you and be

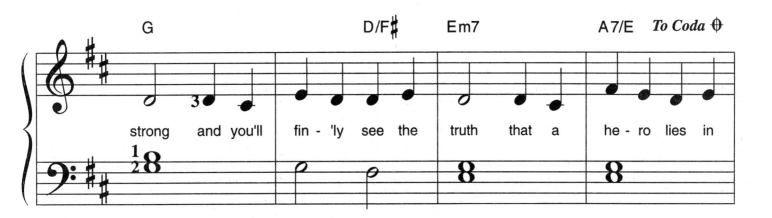

G   D/F♯   Em7   A7/E   *To Coda* ⊕

strong and you'll fin - 'ly see the truth that a he - ro lies in

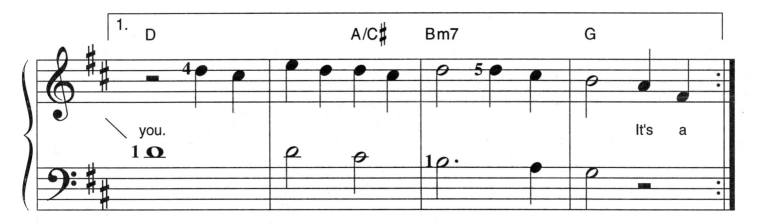

1. D   A/C♯   Bm7   G

you.   It's a

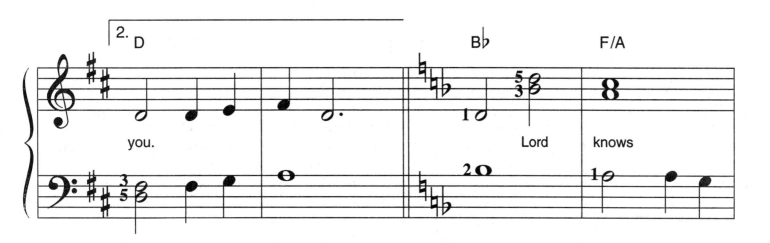

2. D   B♭   F/A

you.   Lord   knows

Hero - 5 - 3

158

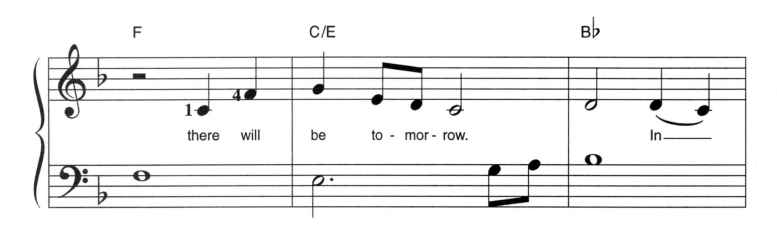

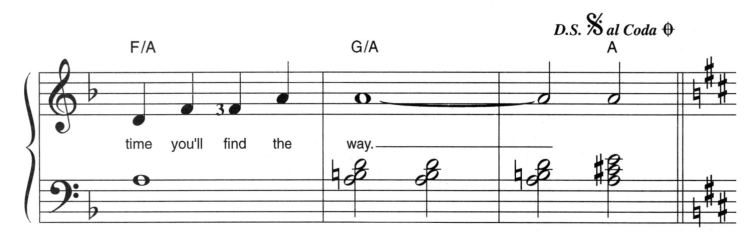

Hero - 5 - 4

Coda

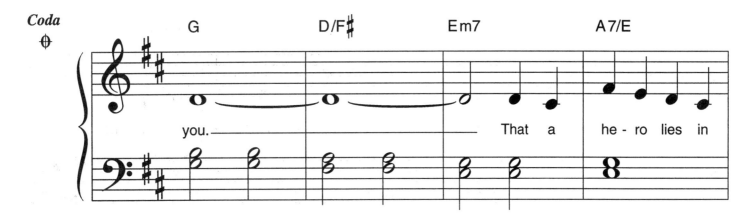

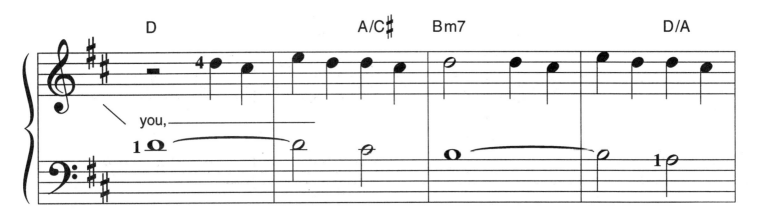

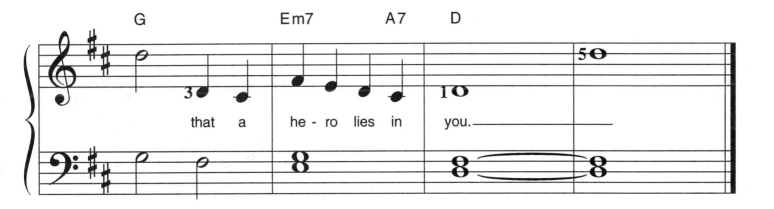

Verse 2:

It's a long road when you face the world alone.
No one reaches out a hand for you to hold.
You can find love if you search with-in yourself
And the emptiness you felt will disappear.

160

THE GIFT

Recorded by Jim Brickman
Featuring Collin Raye and Susan Ashton

Words and Music by
JIM BRICKMAN and TOM DOUGLAS
Arranged by Richard Bradley

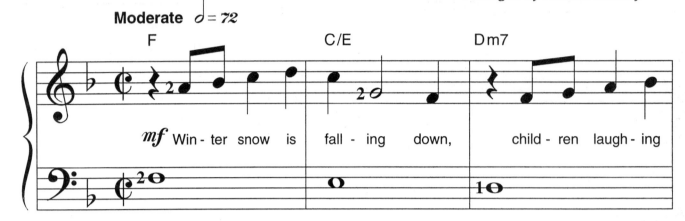

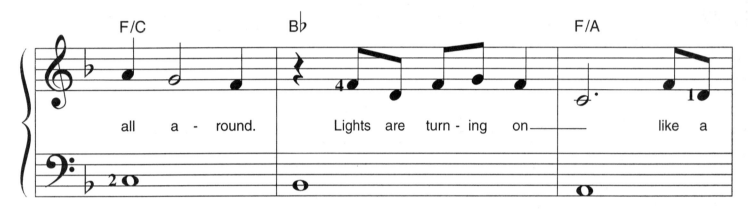

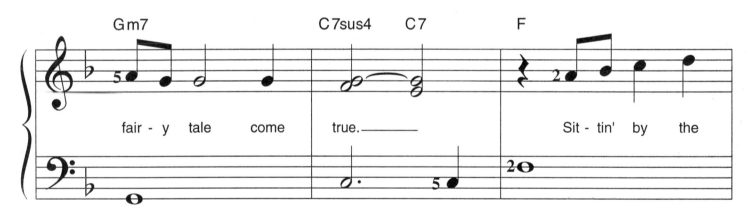

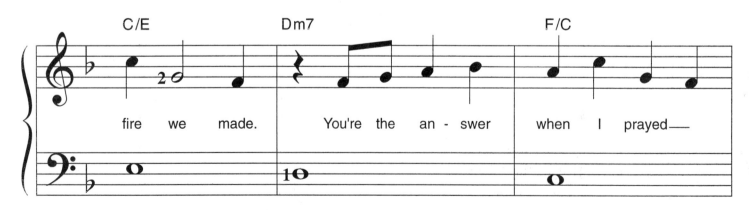

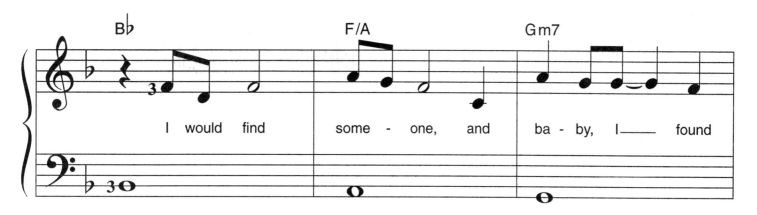

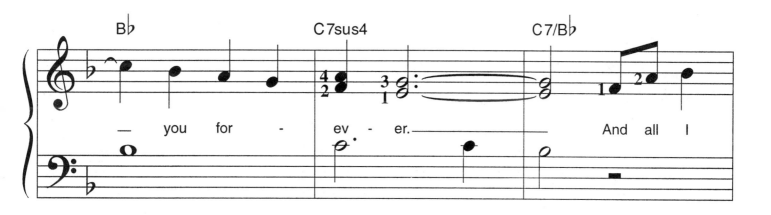

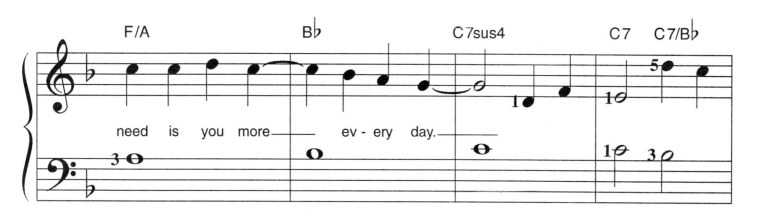

The Gift - 4 - 2

162

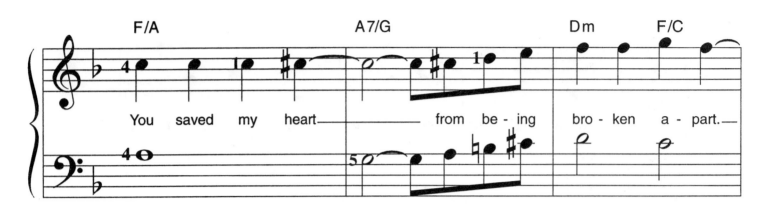

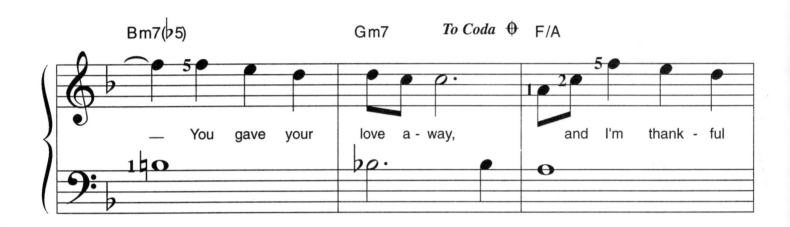

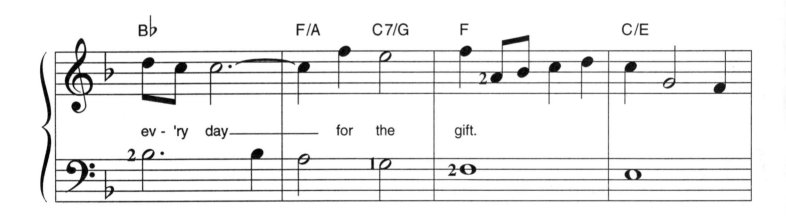

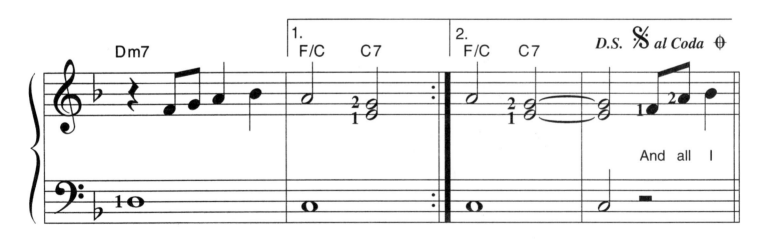

The GIft - 4 - 3

Coda

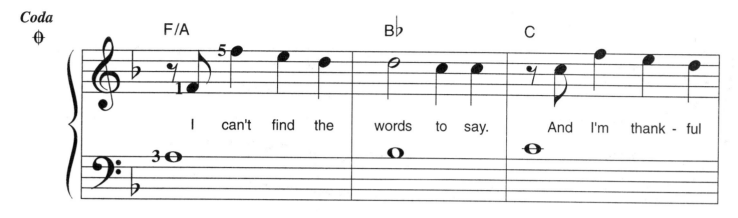

I can't find the words to say. And I'm thank - ful

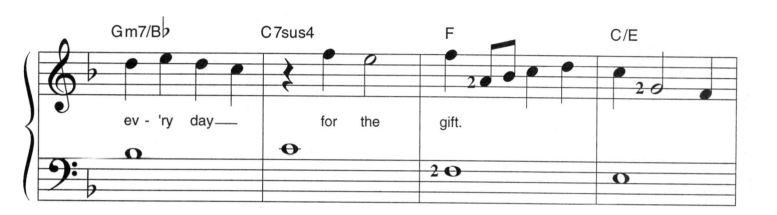

ev - 'ry day— for the gift.

Verse 2:
Watching as you softly sleep.
What I'd give if I could keep just this moment.
If only time stood still.
But the colors fade away
And the years will make us gray.
But baby, in my eyes you'll still be beautiful.
(Chorus:)

YOU MEAN THE WORLD TO ME

Recorded by Toni Braxton

Words and Music by BABYFACE,
L.A. REID and DARYL SIMMONS
Arranged by Richard Bradley

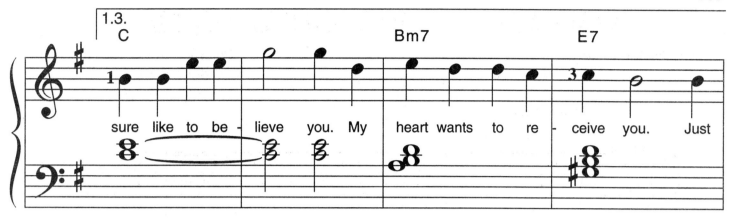

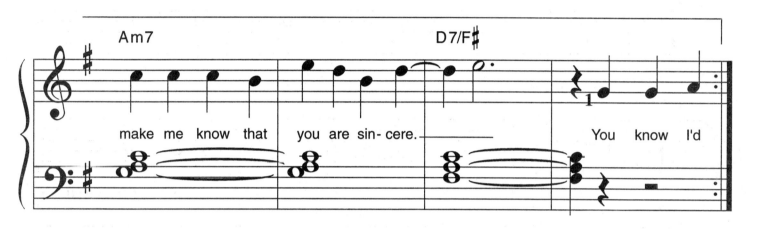

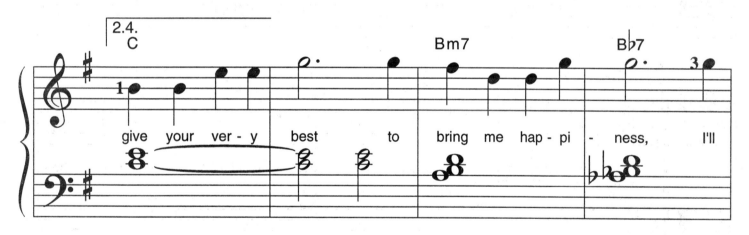

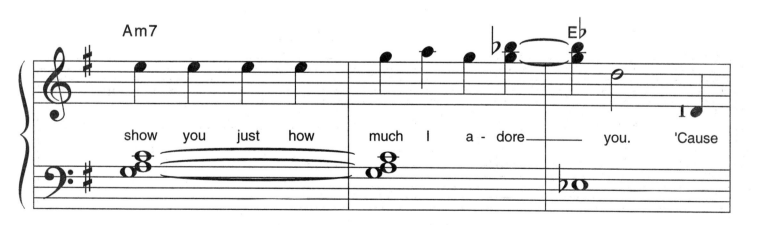

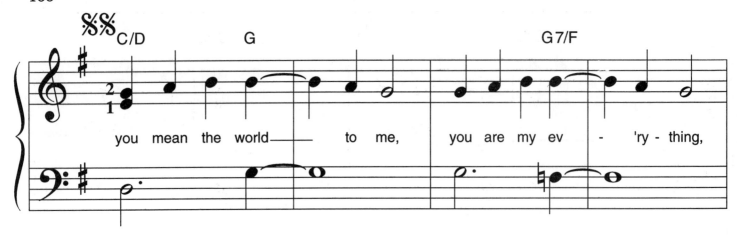

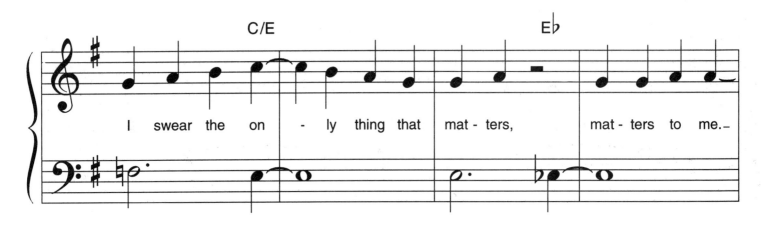

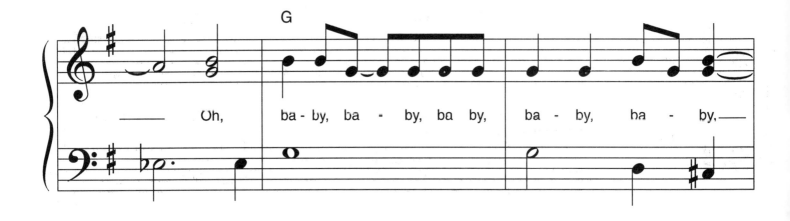

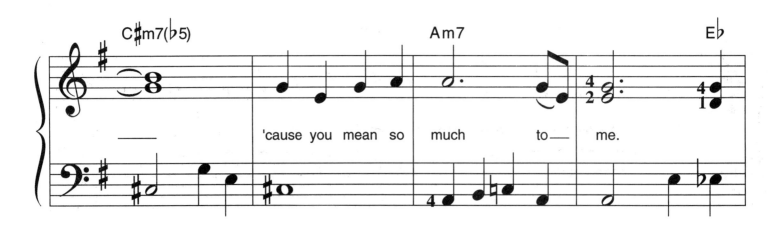

168

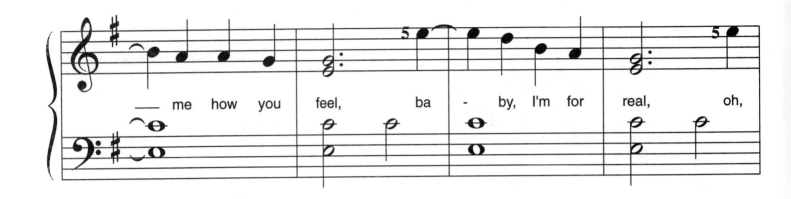

me how you feel, ba - by, I'm for real, oh,

Eb   D.S. %% and fade

ba - by, ba - by, ba - by,   ba - by, ba - by. ___   'Cause

Verse 2:
You know I'd love for you to lead me
And follow through completely,
So won't you give me all I ask for.
And if you give your very best
To bring me happiness
I'll show you just how much I adore you.

Verse 3:
Now it's gonna take some workin'
But I believe you're worth it,
Long as your intentions are good, so good.
There is just one way to show it
And boy, I hope you know it,
That no one could love you like I could.

Verse 4:
Lord knows I want to trust you
And always how I'd love you.
I'm not sure if love is enough.
And I will not be forsaken
And I hope there's no mistakin'.
So tell me that you'll always be true.

I SWEAR

Recorded by All—4—One

Words and Music by
FRANK J. MYERS and GARY BAKER
Arranged by Richard Bradley

I Swear - 5 - 1

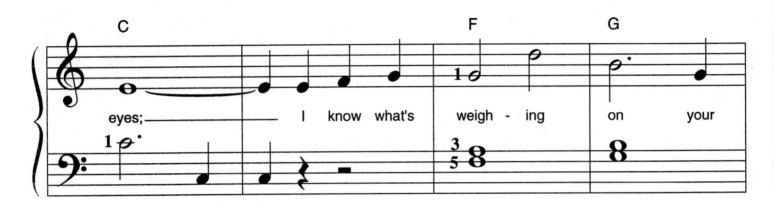

eyes;⸺ I know what's weigh - ing on your

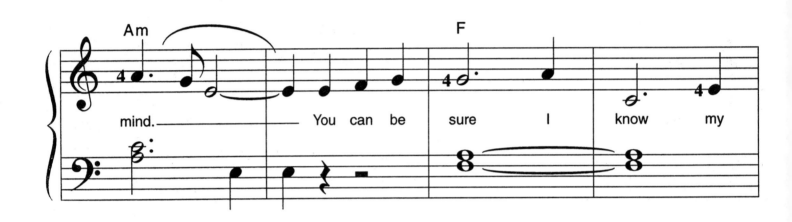

mind.⸺ You can be sure I know my

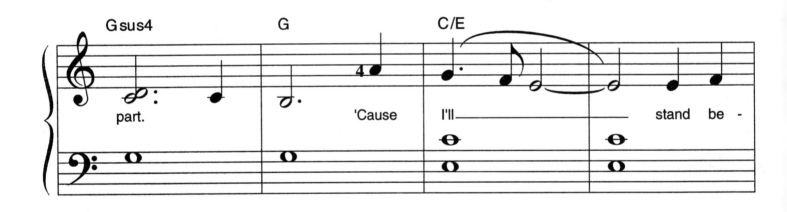

part. 'Cause I'll⸺ stand be -

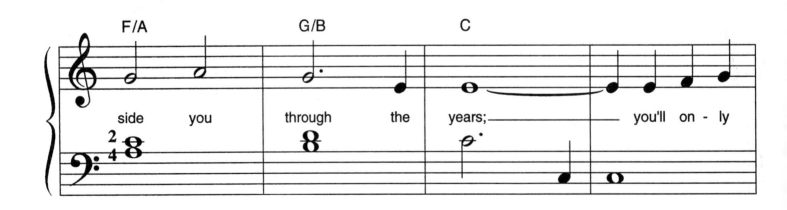

side you through the years;⸺ you'll on - ly

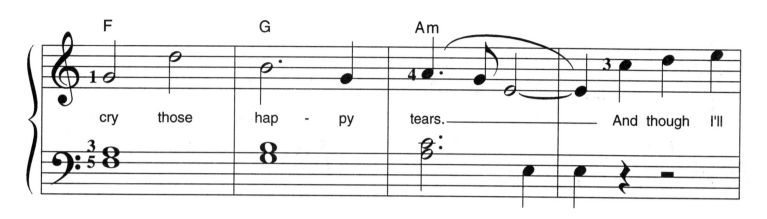

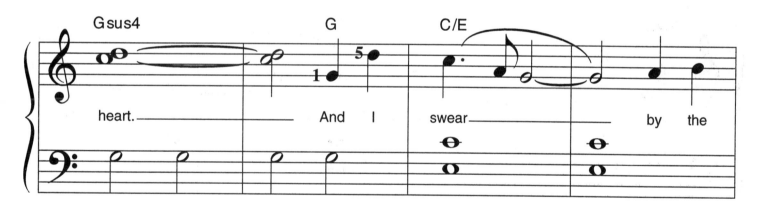

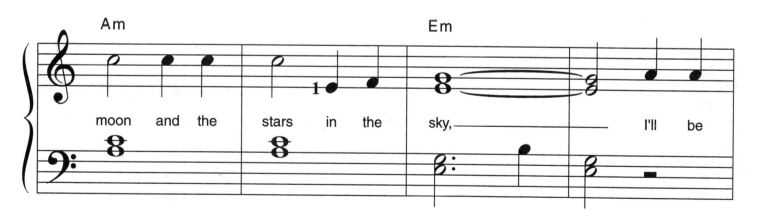

I Swear - 5 - 3

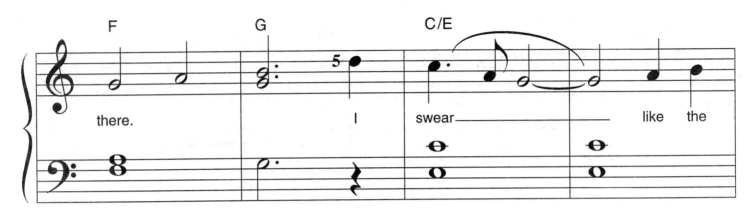

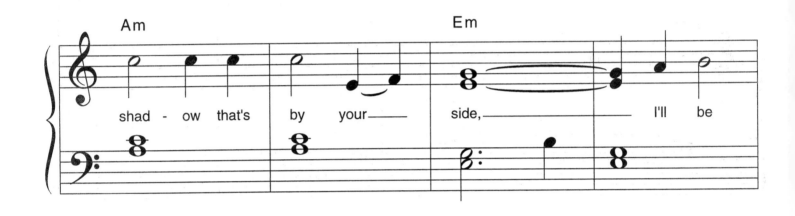

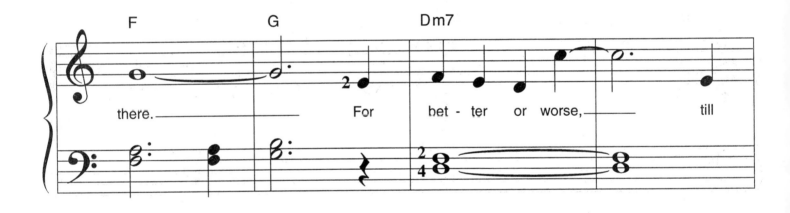

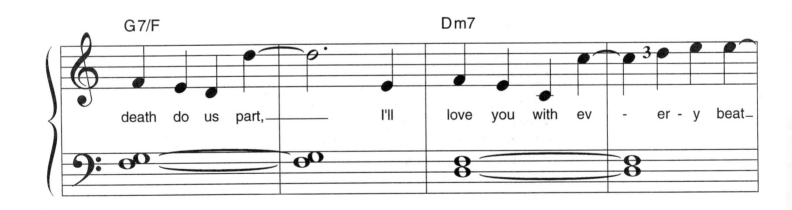

173

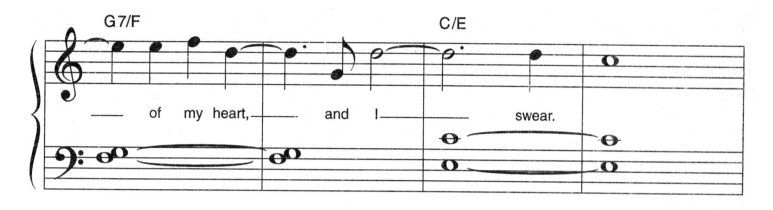

of my heart, _ and I _ swear.

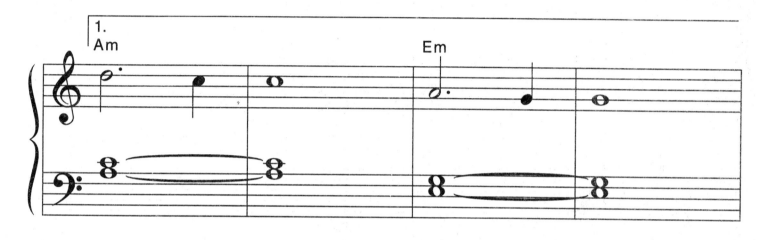

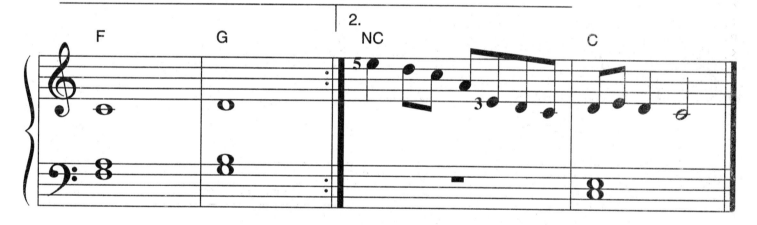

Verse 2:
I'll give you ev'rything I can;
I'll build your dreams with these two hands.
We'll hang some mem'ries on the wall.
And when just the two of us are left,
You won't have to ask if I still care.
'Cause as the time turns the page,
My love won't age at all.

BLUE

Recorded by LeAnn Rimes

Words and Music by
BILL MACK
Arranged by Richard Bradley

175

Blue - 4 - 2

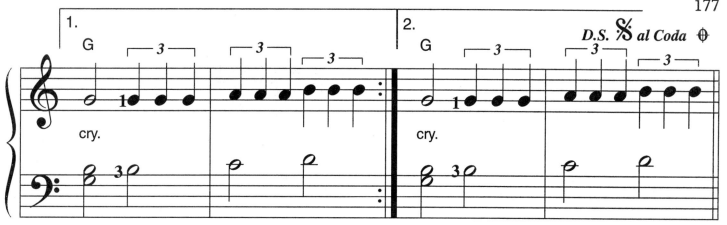

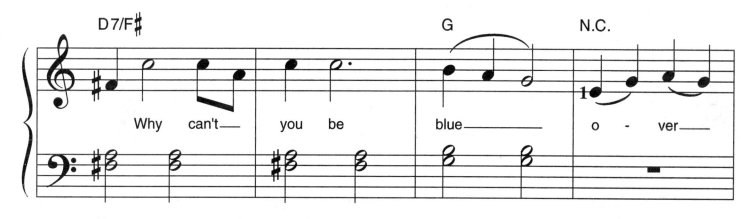

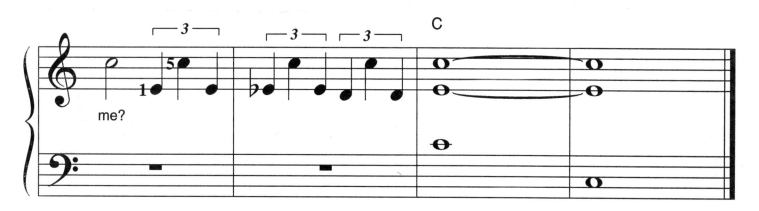

Verse 2:
Now that it's over, I realize
Those sweet words you whispered
Were nothing but lies.
(To Chorus:)

Blue - 4 - 4

(EVERYTHING I DO) I DO IT FOR YOU

From the Motion Picture "Robin Hood: Prince Of Thieves"
Recorded by Bryan Adams

Written by
BRYAN ADAMS, ROBERT JOHN LANGE
and MICHAEL KAMEN
Arranged by Richard Bradley

Slowly ♩ = 64

Look in-to my
Look in-to your

eyes, _____
heart, _____

you ____ will
you ____ will

see _____
find _____

(Everything I Do) I Do It For You - 6 - 1

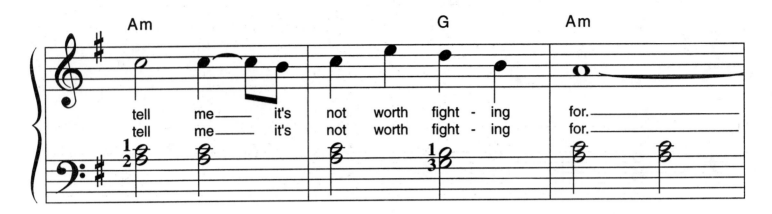

182

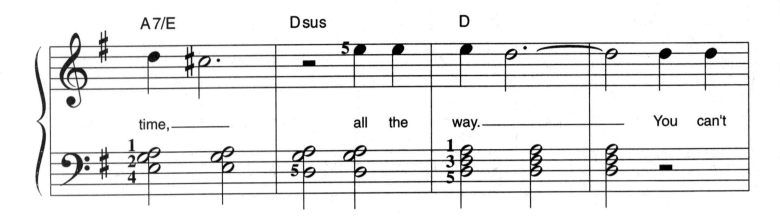

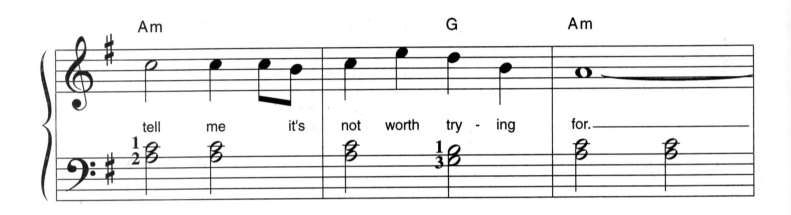

BREAKFAST AT TIFFANY'S

Recorded by Deep Blue Something

Words and Music by
TODD PIPES
Arranged by Richard Bradley

186

Breakfast At Tiffany's - 4 - 3

Verse 2:
I see you, the only one who knew me,
But now your eyes see through me.
I guess I was wrong. So what now?
It's plain to see we're over,
I hate when things are over,
When so much is left undone.
Chorus:

Verse 3:
You'll say we got nothing in common,
No common ground to start from,
And we're falling apart.
You'll say the world has come between us,
Our lives have come between us,
Still I know you just don't care.
Chorus:

DREAMING OF YOU

Recorded by Selena

Words and Music by
TOM SNOW and FRANNE GOLDE
Arranged by Richard Bradley

189

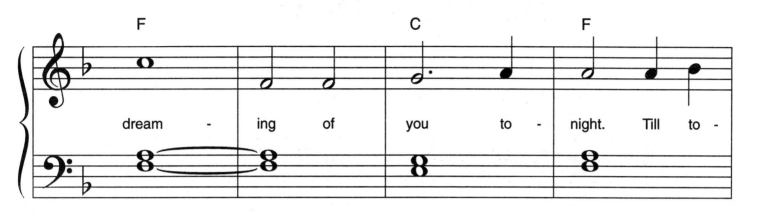

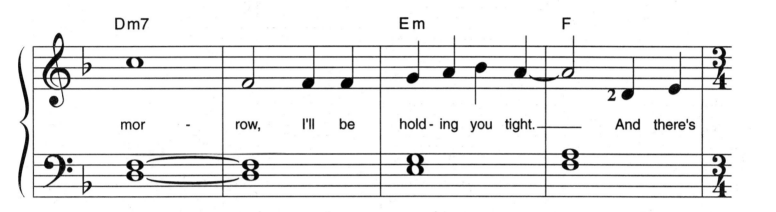

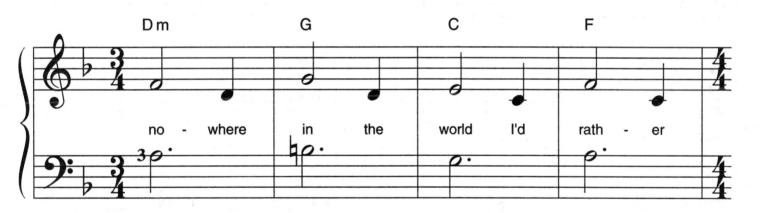

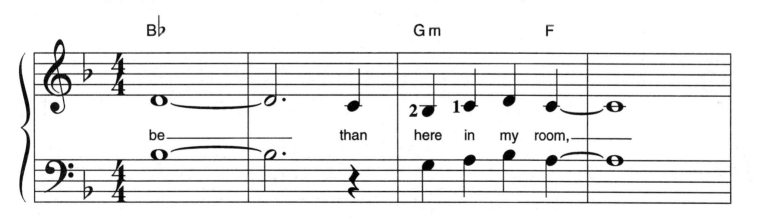

Dreaming Of You - 5 - 2

190

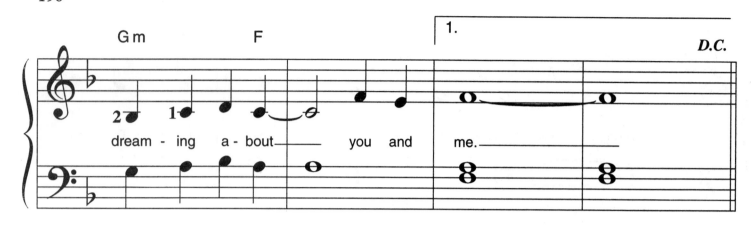

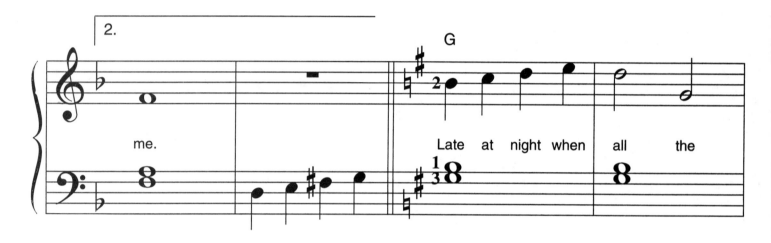

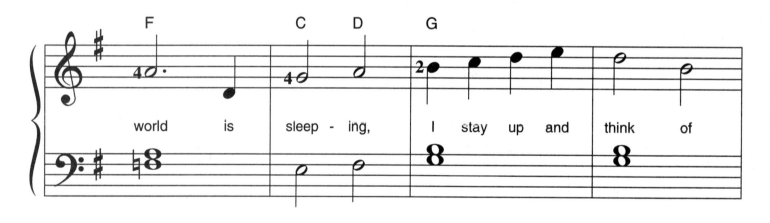

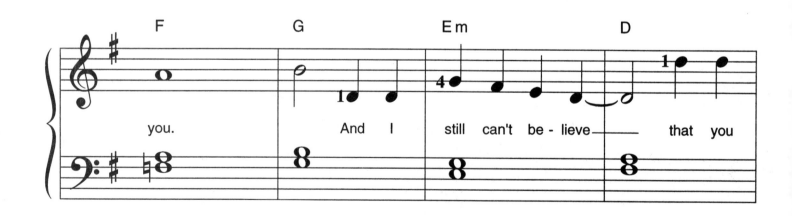

Dreaming Of You - 5 - 3

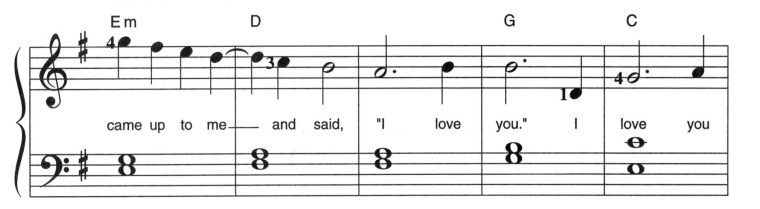

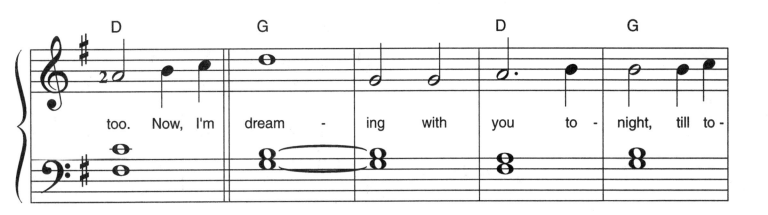

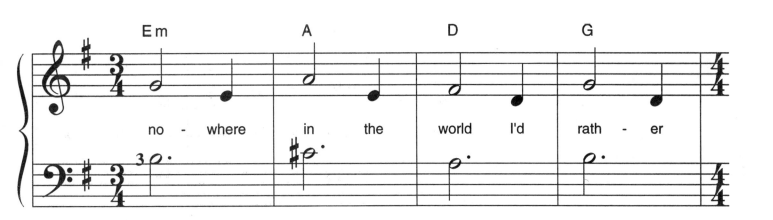

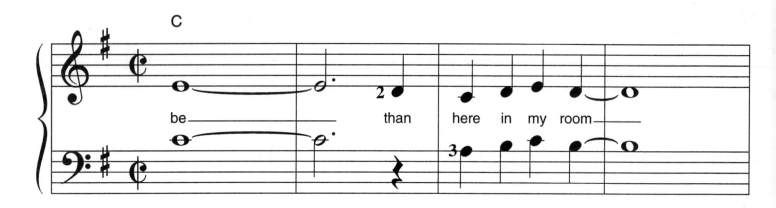

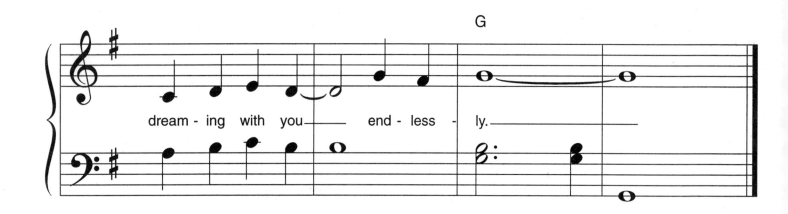

Verse 2:
Wonder if you ever see me
And I wonder if you know I'm there.
If you looked in my eyes,
Would you see what's inside?
Would you even care?

Verse 3:
I just wanna hold you close but so far,
All I have are dreams of you.
So, I wait for the day
And the courage to say
How much I love you.